Advanced Pathfinder 6
Learning through listening

Other titles in the series

CILT, the National Centre for Languages, seeks to support and develop multilingualism and intercultural competence among all sectors of the population in the UK.

CILT is a registered charity, supported by Central Government grants.

advAnced

Pathfinder

6

Learning
through listening

HELEN WRIGHT

The views expressed in this publication are the author's and do not necessarily represent those of CILT, the National Centre for Languages

First published 2004
by CILT, the National Centre for Languages, 20 Bedfordbury, London, WC2N 4LB

Copyright © CILT, the National Centre for Languages 2004

ISBN 1 904243 36 3

A catalogue record for this book is available from the British Library

Printed in Great Britain by Hobbs

CILT Publications are available from: **Central Books**, 99 Wallis Road, London E9 5LN. Tel: 0845 458 9910. Fax: 0845 458 9912. Book trade representation (UK and Ireland): **Broadcast Book Services**, Charter House, 29a London Road, Croydon CR0 2RE. Tel: 020 8681 8949. Fax: 020 8688 0615.

Contents

Introduction

The ability to listen well is essential to achieving a good grade at A level and its importance cannot be underestimated. All too often, however, teachers are uncertain about how they can develop this fundamental skill. This book aims to provide practical support and guidance to enable teachers to approach the teaching of listening with confidence and renewed vigour.

When the listening element of oral examinations is taken into account, up to 50% of an A level in Modern Languages can depend on accurate listening, and an even higher percentage of the preparation that students do in order to prepare for their examinations, to cover the topics and to learn the language, can rely on developing a good ability to listen. This is demonstrated clearly in the Assessment Objectives (AO) which form part of the criteria laid down by QCA and which are a compulsory requirement of all A level specifications:

		AS	A2	A level
AO1	Understand and respond in speech and writing to spoken language	25–35%	20–30%	23–33%
AO2	Understand and respond in speech and writing to written language	25–35%	20–30%	23–33%
AO3	Show knowledge of and apply accurately the prescribed grammar and syntax	25%	25%	25%
AO4	Demonstrate knowledge and understanding of aspects of the chosen society	10–20%	20–30%	12–25%

Each of these Assessment Objectives relates in some way to listening:

- AO1 demands understanding of the spoken word and the ability to respond to it;
- AO2 requires students to be able to discuss texts with an examiner and, naturally, to be able to understand and respond to further oral questions;
- AO3 asks for accuracy in the spoken word, which again involves interaction and conversation;
- AO4 emphasises the need for students to build up a good understanding of the target-language society, much of which will be available to them through listening – to native speakers, to the radio, to satellite broadcasts and simply by listening while they are visiting the country themselves.

Learning through listening aims, then, to allow teachers to understand more comprehensively the skill and art of listening, and to help them as a result to plan and develop more effectively useful strategies for the advanced level classroom. Exposure to the spoken language and tasks which involve listening practice are the standard mainstays of development in most A level listening skills lessons. These activities form a central part of the strategies explored throughout the book. However, the text also delves deeper into what we know about listening in a foreign language, looking at what research can tell us about the development of listening skills, and appreciating how teachers might use these insights to organise a staged programme to improve listening skills at advanced level.

The book is divided into four chapters. Chapter 1 looks at the skill of listening and explores research that has been done into listening by both first and second language learners. Listening is a receptive skill, but 'receptive' should not be taken to mean 'passive'. Listening is a highly active process and this understanding flows throughout the book. It explores a wide range of difficulties faced by students who are still learning to listen in a second language and looks at some practical solutions to emerge from research, notably the importance of developing in our students an awareness of the different aspects of listening and the variety of strategies that they can practise and use. This is a prelude to Chapter 2, which looks more closely at the challenges faced by students who have just completed their language GCSEs and who are embarking on post-16 study. Chapter 2 outlines the goals that we must set our students, and looks closely at the skills and strategies they will need to develop to reach a good level of fluency in listening by A2. Guidance is given about how to present these listening strategies as part of a programme of developing strategy awareness to help students see how they can improve their own listening.

Chapter 3 explores how teachers can select appropriate material and prepare tasks to form part of a programme to improve listening. Ideas for potential sources of texts and tasks are given, together with guidance on evaluating progress and integrating listening into an overall scheme of work. The emphasis is on providing ideas to help students take responsibility for their own learning and practice, and to help give them a good grounding in the skills involved in listening that will enable them to continue to make independent progress beyond the classroom.

Finally, Chapter 4 gives specific advice about preparing for the A level examination, including hints, tips and guidance for students on how they can best prepare themselves practically and psychologically for the day of their listening and oral examinations. This is a practical chapter which will be of direct and immediate use for students and teachers in the last stages of an A level course. Thorough development of listening techniques over time is by far the best way to prepare for the examination, but all these skills need to be brought together and teachers will find the advice given in this chapter invaluable in encouraging their students over the final hurdle.

The ideas and strategies presented throughout the book are not intended to be narrowly specific to the GCE. Teachers of SCE Higher Grade examinations and Irish Honours Leaving Certificate will find almost all of the material directly relevant to the courses followed by their students, while teachers of vocational language courses will find the sections on strategy awareness and range of texts and tasks of particular interest. Case studies illustrate a range of effective classroom practice in different contexts that improve listening in the classroom. Photocopiable checklists and resource sheets for students and teachers throughout the book (marked **S** for students and **T** for teachers) are a useful source of information that can be transferred directly to the classroom. Direct links to the websites mentioned in the book are provided in the Web page accompanying *Learning through listening*: **www.cilt.org.uk/publications/ learningthroughlistening**. Ultimately, we all share the same goal: we want to ensure that our students learn to listen as fluently as they can and as quickly and as effectively as possible. This book will help teachers make this happen.

1

What is listening?

What research tells us

Research into listening, particularly in the past 30 years, has provided us with a much clearer picture of what the skill of listening in a second language actually involves. It is worth spending a little time investigating the findings of this research, as it gives us an important – and fascinating – insight into the complexity of a skill we often assume 'just happens'. We will then be in a much better position to help our students understand what they need to do in order to improve their listening and be much more able to plan how we can help them do so.

What do we do when we listen?

Listening is not the same as hearing. Hearing is a neurological process that enables the brain to recognise sound as sound; deaf people lack this ability and cannot hear. Listening, on the other hand, is a set of neurological and cognitive processes that enable the hearer to decode and make sense of speech. When we listen, we 'receive, attend to and assign meaning to' what we hear (Oxford 1993).

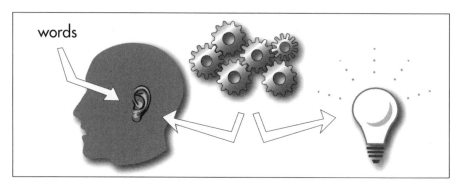
words

We might legitimately say that the term 'listening comprehension' is tautological, but we use it in practice to distinguish the **action** of understanding the spoken language from the **attempt** to understand the spoken language, i.e. the uncompleted action. When people say 'he listened hard but could not work out what she was saying', they are not referring to our interpretation of the term 'listening comprehension' – listening in a foreign language means to us the act of concentration on, or attention to, speech, with the intention of understanding meaning.

Successful listening, then, results in understanding – and whether they are successful or only partially successful, advanced learners of a second language engage in a wide range of processes to enable them to understand the spoken word. Different ways have been used by researchers to describe these processes involved in listening: Wilkinson et al (1974), in their investigation of listening for the Schools Oracy Project, describe a number of means by which the human brain decodes spoken communication, including:

- linguistic (the words and syntax);
- paralinguistic (how the language is spoken – register, intonation, etc);
- visual (what we can pick up from what we can see or read).

Given that most of the texts our learners encounter in the examinations are oral recordings accompanying written examinations, these are the three ways of understanding that are of most interest to us as teachers, although we should not underestimate in teaching listening what Penny Ur (1984: 5) describes as 'environmental clues'. In face-to-face interaction in the foreign language, or in watching video and satellite, we understand a lot more when we look at facial expressions, body movements and reactions, just as we do when we listen to people speaking in our mother tongue. This, of course, is why it is easier to understand nuances when we have a direct conversation rather than a conversation over the telephone. If we can train our students to look for these clues, too, they will have an advantage in learning to understand the spoken word more quickly.

From micro to macro – listening as a set of cognitive processes

Listening happens on various levels: at the most micro level of listening is the distinction between individual sounds, while at the macro level the listener must comprehend subtext, or meaning that is not necessarily directly expressed in the combination of words that make up speech. In between, a number of processes are involved, not all of which will necessarily be used concurrently, but which together make up the skill of listening. Distinction of sounds alone will not lead to understanding of meaning, unless the speech consists only of unconnected phonemes, and the only meaning that can be derived is that of unconnected sound; comprehension of subtext will be impossible without an understanding of words, syntax and sense.

Listening – and particularly listening at an advanced level – consists of all of these skills, and Rost (1991) helpfully draws the skills of listening identified by research into the following list:

- *perception skills:*
  – discriminating between sounds;
  – recognising words.

- *analysis skills:*
  – identifying syntactical clues;
  – identifying 'pragmatic' clues, i.e. patterns of words like set
    expressions and utterances.

- *synthesis skills:*
  – connecting of linguistic to paralinguistic and non-linguistic
    clues;
  – using of schemata, the background information;
  – recalling concepts.

Successful listening combines a 'bottom-up' approach, based on working out meaning as a result of auditory perception, with a 'top-down' approach to understanding meaning, based on perception of words **after** their meaning has been understood by the listener. As Kelly (1991: 135) neatly summarises it:

> *The bottom-up is the sound input and the top-down is the application of cognitive faculties. The mind sets up the expectations and the sound provides confirmation. Perception occurs when sufficient information has been provided from both sources.*

Brown (1986: 293) describes effective listening in similar terms as:

> *actively seeking to construct a coherent, self-consistent mental representation, and [...] actively seeking to eliminate inconsistencies from that representation.*

In this active construction, the role of the listener's knowledge of the universe (and the particular aspects of the universe about which the speaker is speaking) is crucial, and as teachers we need to be aware of this wider picture as we set about encouraging our students to learn to become better listeners. Most importantly, we have to realise – and set about persuading our students – that listening is an active process and not one that can be taken for granted.

How do we listen? Insights for the teacher of a foreign language

Successful listening involves using together all of the skills listed above. Listening is a dynamic process: good listeners will identify which skills they need for different types of listening and will call on them almost automatically as and when required. Our task as teachers is to encourage both the development of these various skills and to enable learners to learn how to use them together and instantaneously. Researchers have discovered some interesting insights into how this learning to listen actually happens.

Words not sounds

As listeners, we are able to distinguish sounds from one another because of the difference in their loudness, their length and the frequency on which they are emitted, and, clearly, auditory perception is an important primary stage in the comprehension process. Although it is tempting, as teachers, to want to build the skill of listening from the individual sound unit upwards, research indicates that in fact we are able to distinguish groups of sounds as easily as the individual sounds themselves as shown in, for example, research by Liberman (1970). Words are groups of sounds – not just a sound segment but a sound segment **with meaning**, and this suggests that it is not just the sound that listeners hear but simultaneously the meaning. This is the first element of interest for teachers – we need not feel obliged to practise phoneme discrimination divorced from meaning – when we teach a word together with the accurate pronunciation of its sounds, we also teach how to recognise that word spoken by a native speaker and how to discriminate between words that sound nearly the same.

Selective attention

Another interesting finding to emerge from research is that while the ability to distinguish or recognise sounds and hence words is a necessary component of listening, this does not imply that the listener pays the same amount of **attention** to every word produced in speech. Attention is a crucial feature in the listening process and in distinguishing listening from hearing, and evidence suggests that we are able to choose what linguistic input we pay attention to in listening. Treisman (1960, 1964), for example, discovered in his investigation of the effects of loudness, voice quality and meaning on how subjects select what to listen to, found that listeners can, by attending to the quality of the input, 'shadow' a voice of one sex and ignore the other when two voices of similar loudness are presented to the listener. When the voices are distinguished by their loudness or softness, again the listener is able to attend to either by choice. This has implications for the teaching of listening – if we can encourage our students to be aware that they do not have to pay attention to everything they hear, they will become more efficient listeners.

Prediction

Other research suggests that we employ decoding processes that depend on prediction of meaningful information that is yet to be received. These cognitive decoding processes must, if the information has not yet been received by the listener, therefore draw on existing knowledge held by the listener to construct, as he/she listens, a representation of the knowledge that has been, is being and will probably be communicated by the speaker. There are obviously levels of understanding of this knowledge – Vanderplank (1988), for example, describes experiments that set out to assess levels of intelligibility in response to exercises requiring listening. Native speakers distinguished between two psychologically real categories of 'following' and 'understanding', where the latter is a more central form of complete listening than the former. The research revealed that, unlike non-native speakers, native speakers are able to choose in their listening whether simply to 'follow' or to 'understand'. In a situation where the listener has sufficient decoding processes available to him/her, but chooses simply to follow rather than to understand, the role of attention as a determiner of meaning is clear. However, in a situation where the listener has no choice but to follow rather than to understand, this can be interpreted as either insufficiently developed decoding processes – phonological or cognitive – to receive and anticipate meaning, or insufficient existing world knowledge.

This of course lends weight to our belief as teachers in the importance of **background schemata** – the essential cultural knowledge that our learners need to gain in order to be able to understand what is going on around them. Particularly in the case of listening, where other clues may be limited, background knowledge is crucial to the successful understanding of what is being said, and we need to encourage our students not only to develop their general knowledge of the foreign language country, but to engage in guesswork – for example, if the speaker is talking about a current political issue, what stance might he or she be taking, and why?

Interactive listening

As teachers, we must not forget that in the comprehension of speech, listening will usually involve **interaction** with other people – the speakers. In this dynamic interaction there is also to be found contextual meaning that extends beyond the surface meaning of the words and syntax. There is useful research which shows the importance of movements and gestures in reinforcing phonological or discourse features of the speaker's language, in controlling the interaction and in conveying the linguistic message. When Riseborough (1981) investigated the use of gestures, she discovered that they aided comprehension significantly and compensated for the introduction of 'noise' – speech patterns that were difficult to decode because of their auditory opaqueness. Beyond simply adding clues to meaning, however, interaction can bring new meaning. Rinvolucri (1981) describes a technique he calls 'empathetic listening', where the listener, by attempting to empathise strongly with what the speaker is saying, is actually able to encourage the speaker to give more information and add to the meaning communicated to the listener. Muddled thoughts can be clarified through talking and listening to the prompts of other people; what Kleist (1805) draws together neatly in the image *l'idée vient en parlant.*

What makes listening hard

The factors that cause interference in listening are significant because they give us an insight into what to be aware of as the learner develops the skills involved in listening – strategies for successful listening at any level, but especially at an advanced level, where the texts are usually more complex, will need to include strategies to cope with the interference factors. Penny Ur (1984) describes a number of difficulties that language learners encounter when they listen in their second language:

- *hearing (or not hearing) sounds that do not occur in their first language;*
- *coping with unfamiliar stress and intonation patterns;*

- *managing to find sense in a message despite redundancy and noise;*
- *listening when tired;*
- *understanding different accents;*
- *interpreting non-linguistic clues.*

Teachers need to be aware of these difficulties if they are to understand why some students find listening a challenge. Similarly, it is helpful to be aware of Rubin's (1994) list of five main factors that affect listening comprehension, as identified in a wide-ranging review of listening comprehension research.

Text characteristics: when spoken utterances are faster and less distinct, comprehension is more difficult and when texts are particularly dense, again, comprehension is more difficult. Type of text too affects comprehension – narrative texts are easier to recall than expository texts, and texts that follow a chronological order are easier to comprehend than non-chronologically ordered texts. This reflects the fact that construction of meaning by the listener will be significantly more possible if the listener has already the world view that the speaker possesses.

Interlocutor characteristics: Markham (1988), for instance, describes research that suggests different degrees of recall by listeners depending on the gender of the speaker. How much we understand and retain when listening is certainly affected by our relationship with the speaker, and we need to be aware of this.

Task characteristics: these affect listening in as much as the cues in the text can interfere with or encourage comprehension. Different tasks require different types of listening: tasks may demand that the listener listens for detail, paying selective attention to specific items, or for gist, or critically to analyse and evaluate arguments. Alternatively, they may demand focus on emotional content or to gain a sensory impression. Failure to identify (consciously or otherwise) and use the processes required for the specific task faced by the listener is likely to mean that the listener understands less of what is being said.

Listener characteristics: language proficiency level and knowledge of the world are key determiners in effective listening.

Process characteristics: there is research to show that listening is affected by the processes that the listeners use and the strategies that they employ. Van Patten (1989), for example, describes evidence to suggest that when less expert listeners are required to listen for a morpheme or a key word (bottom-up processing) as well as meaning (top-down processing), their understanding of content is restricted, suggesting that they are less able to process overall meaning than individual words, and are more restricted in their use of strategy. O'Malley et al (1989) discovered that effective listeners used more self-monitoring, elaboration and inferencing than ineffective listeners, and this is a key area which we will explore at the end of this chapter and in Chapter 2.

There is clearly a difference between how people listen, and this affects how well the meaning is extracted from the message, and if we can identify key effective strategies that our students should be using, then we will be much more able to guide them towards better listening.

As teachers, we need to be as aware as possible of the potential difficulties faced by advanced learners so that we can help to minimise their effect, both in how we plan our listening skills programme and in how we prepare our students. At the two ends of the listening spectrum – micro and macro skills – a few simple steps can make an immediate difference in two of the key areas identified above, namely background cultural information and difficult sound features. Exam-board specifications list in detail the cultural areas they expect students to cover in the course of their studies and these are a good starting point for a development of cultural awareness and an understanding of which schemata need extending. The following photocopiable checklist, meanwhile, provides a starting point for both teachers and students as regards difficult sounds.

---

1 **T** **S** checklist

Challenging sound features – be on your guard!

If you are aware of the following sound features, and listen out for them, you will find that when you listen to second language speakers their conversation makes much more sense.

All languages

- colloquialisms, slang and shortened forms;
- 'false friends' – words that sound like English but have a different meaning and whose similarities need to be highlighted when they are first learned, for example:
  - *ignorer*, not to know, to be unaware of;
  - *eventuell*, possibly;
  - *sensible*, sensitive
- word order, which can differ from English for reasons of grammar, emphasis or style.

© CILT, the National Centre for Languages 2004

Challenging sound features – be on your guard (contd)

French

- accentuation, which goes by the sentence rather than the word, so stresses will not always appear in the same place for each word you hear;
- silent letters – words are not written as they sound, so the visual/auditory link in your mind will be weaker;
- compound tenses – listen out for both parts (auxiliary and participle);
- negation, which involves two parts – listen out for both the *ne* and the *pas/rien/jamais* etc which actually defines the meaning;
- *liaisons and enchaînement* – this means that words often run into one another;
- sounds which do not appear in English: R apical (pronounced in the throat), nasal vowels, and the subtle (to untrained ears) differences between **tu/tous** and parl**é**/parl**ais**.

German

- long sentences – these can be a challenge to follow, particularly when you are listening out for the verb at the end;
- compound tenses, which are common;
- long, often compound, words – these need careful unpicking;
- sounds which do not appear in English: many of the vowel sounds, especially the Umlaut sounds and dipthongs, the R sound, the Scottish 'ch'.

Russian

- the strong syllable stress – unstressed syllables are often only faintly heard during rapid speech;
- word order – this may be significantly different from the expected English order;
- filler words: the spoken language is characterised by various types of filler word, e.g. значит and little modal particles, e.g. ведь, же and interjections, e.g. ах!
- compound words – there are many of these, both nouns and verbs, formed upon significant roots;
- changes of stress and vowel: familiar words may become very unfamilar because of significant changes of stress and vowel, either in oblique cases, e.g. отéц – genitive отцá, or between singular and plural, e.g. сестрá – plural сёстры.

Spanish

- subject pronouns – these are usually dropped, so you must know and listen out for the verb conjugation to know who or what is being referred to;
- the subjunctive, which is much more common than in English and is used regularly after many different conjunctions, e.g. *que, cuando, como*, etc – be aware of it and listen out for it;
- sounds which do not appear in English: the rolled R, the J (similar to the French R), and the B/V.

How do learners become better listeners?

Knowing what the difficulties are is one thing; learning to overcome them is another. But there is plenty of research evidence available to set teachers and students on the right track.

Out of the mouths of babes ...

Research, for example Oxford (1993), shows that the younger first language listener is in many ways similar to a low proficiency second language listener and one of the most important findings to emerge from research into listening in children learning their **first** language is that our advanced language learners already possess many of the strategies that will enable them to become good listeners.

Cutler and Swinney (1987), for example, report on the results of four experiments conducted to test the ability of children between the ages of four and six, and six and eight to listen to and respond (by pressing a button) to target words in sentences. The bank of words used contained both content and function words. Each word was presented in two sentences – one in which it was the most prominent word by virtue of it receiving the primary sentence accent, and one in which it was unaccented. To ensure that the children were in fact processing the sentences, and not simply hearing the words, only children that passed a comprehension test were included in the results. The reaction times of the children to the word were noted, and the longer reaction times observed for function words revealed that both groups of children found function words difficult to process. An explanation for this, namely the nature of the listening processing strategies available to children, was revealed by this series of experiments. Although one of the experiments showed that all of the children were sensitive to stress on words when the words were presented in non-syntactic lists, the younger children were unable to respond more quickly to sentences in which the word was accented, while the older group showed a time advantage in response to accented words, indicating that they had been able to develop by this stage a listening strategy that took account of the semantic focus of a sentence. A similar experiment with stories – continuous prose as opposed to isolated sentences – using adult controls as well as the groups of younger and older children, gave similar results.

The importance of cognitive and meta-cognitive strategies

We can conclude from this that advanced listening needs cognitive strategies which develop over time, but also that our students already possess – in their first language – the strategies they will need to be good listeners in a foreign language. We can certainly focus on this in a programme to develop advanced listening skills: while beginning learners of a second language must learn to perceive sound and rhythmic patterns, similar to the processes of learning first language listening (Byrnes 1984), as they become more proficient, their task is to develop top-down as well as bottom-up processing of text, drawing on context and background knowledge (Richards 1983). A second language learner is likely to have more background world knowledge than a first language learner, but he or she still has to develop knowledge of the characteristics of language that help enable prediction of text – lexical and structural clues – and will have to develop social and cultural awareness of non-verbal clues to meaning. The learner will also have to adjust his or her own cognitive representations of time and space to match those expressed in the target language, and planned exposure in an advanced level course to a wide range of contextual information, both linguistic and cultural, will naturally help our students to improve their listening skills.

A second language listener has an additional strategy at his or her disposal – translation. Evidence provided by Eastman (1991), however, suggests that part of the cognitive development required of the second language learner of listening (who in the early stages beyond sound recognition needs to rely on translation as his or her main source of comprehension) is to move away from 'on-line' translation as a main listening process. Translation, after all, cannot adequately communicate more than the surface features of the message. Evidence collected by Hayashi (1991) suggests that the use of top-down processing in listening comprehension by second language listeners is hindered by lexical inadequacies, namely lack of word recognition. Kelly (1991) describes research into the type of error made by a near-native learner of language transcribing spoken language and notes that while perceptual, syntactical and lexical errors were all in evidence, those caused by ignorance of lexis formed a significantly high proportion of the total. Students need to be constantly reminded, then, that vocabulary learning is essential to the art of effective listening, but that vocabulary alone will not make them good listeners.

Improving memory processes improves listening ability in longer discourse (Oxford 1990), while listeners who wish to become more effective must learn what kind of listening they are expected to do as a result of what the task requires of them (Oxford 1993). O'Malley et al (1989), in their investigation of strategies used by effective and ineffective listeners, discovered that not only do more effective listeners use a higher level of cognitive process in establishing the meaning of text – they listen for larger portions of text; they use top-down, inferencing strategies unless difficulties in sound perception prevent them from doing so, in which case they switch immediately to bottom-up strategies; they elaborate on text heard by using their own knowledge and self-questioning – they are also able to direct these strategies when they are aware of lack of comprehension. Just as they are aware of their attention and are able consciously to redirect attention when it is affected by fatigue, they are able to manipulate their use of strategies in the most appropriate way to enable comprehension of the text. By so doing, they are in fact making their use of strategy more automatic and are becoming better listeners.

What can research into improving reading tell us about listening?

Similar evidence is to be found in reading research – Tang and Moore (1992), for example, relate research that suggests that when readers are actively encouraged to use cognitive and metacognitive strategies prior to reading a text, their comprehension of the text improves and, significantly, so does their comprehension of texts they read later (when the readers are not specifically encouraged, as in the initial test situation, to treat the texts in a particular way).

The field of research into reading gives us even more clues as to how learners can improve their listening, as reading can be compared to listening – reading, like listening, is a receptive skill, decoding language received. Despite the differences between the types of input received by the reader and the listener, there are significant similarities, particularly in the cognitive processes that are used to understand both types of text. Written language is read at the pace the reader determines rather than heard at the pace the speaker speaks and usually consists of complete, tightly organised, grammatical structures in which the phonological element is missing; listening usually involves more immediate and visible interaction between listener and speaker, and the texts are often shorter, with redundant utterances and 'noise'. The processing strategies used to decode both, however, are very similar.

Research into how learners learn to become better readers, then, also helps us understand how they can become better listeners. Gerrig and Murphy (1992), for example, describe four experiments to test the comprehension of new (that is to say, invented) compound nouns that required the readers to recognise a general relationship between two categories. When they investigated the time taken by the subjects to read and understand the new compounds in texts where the meaning was implicit and explicit, they concluded that the best readers *actively use the context* in forming concepts like *'vodka face'* (Gerrig and Murphy 1992: 228).

Noordman and Vonk (1992) investigated the inferences made by readers about causal relations in texts with familiar and unfamiliar topics. Their conclusion was that readers needed background knowledge to be able to make the inference, even if the relation was made explicit in the text.

Evidence from reading research suggests that second language readers can transfer skills from first language reading capability – Koda (1988), for example, describes two experiments that investigated how four groups of readers from different language backgrounds (Arabic, English, Japanese and Spanish) reacted to the blocking of certain sounds and the introduction of homophones into text. She discovered that readers reacted in line with the expectations of how they retrieved information in their first language. This evidence suggests in turn that second language listeners may be able to access first language listening strategies, although this transfer will be restricted in the beginning stages of listening in a second language by perception of sound and understanding of new lexis in the second language, which lead the listener to build up new frameworks of meaning as they listen. This certainly supports the evidence gathered in the listening research discussed above, and extends our understanding of the cognitive processes involved in listening.

Strategies for improving listening

Obviously, as teachers of second language listening, we want our learners to be able to develop to the highest possible level the cognitive processes that will enable them to understand well, not just to follow. In a group of words other than a list, the combined meaning of all the words forms a unit of meaning, and it is the decoding of this meaning that is the essential goal of the listener. Individual words, although they form part of the whole meaning of the phrase or sentence are less important than the meaning of the whole. Langs (1978) draws this all together and categorises listening as having three realms:

- the cognitive – i.e. the brain processes required to make sense of the components of language used in listening – words, sounds, intonation, etc;
- the object relational – i.e. the context of the language, which must be appreciated for the text to be understood;
- the interactional – i.e. the dynamic process of creation and understanding of meaning which happens when one person talks to another.

If we can make our students **aware** of this, they will have a much better chance of being effective listeners, and our goal should be to allow them access to the strategies for good listening that they already possess. As they attempt to create meaning, i.e. comprehend the sense of the spoken utterances, they will make inferences about the content and sense of what they are hearing by using a number of strategies, for example judging the sense of references made by the speaker, supplying links between lexical items to confirm the semantic relation, using cultural schemata, supporting data and genre to fill the gaps of 'understood' material, and interpreting the speaker's intention or purpose in speaking.

Significant work on researching and identifying these strategies more precisely and on extending them into a typology has been done by O'Malley and Chamot (1987) and O'Malley et al (1989), and it is these strategies that we will want to adapt to help us to teach the skill of learning to listen. Barry Jones (2001) looks in detail at learning strategies in his book Advanced Pathfinder 2: *Developing learning strategies*, and much of what follows draws on similar research into learning. In fact, this comprehensive list of strategies will form the basis of the strategy training described in Chapter 2, and is referred to throughout the book. Here, the strategies are presented as a list for reference and to prompt reflection.

Learning to listen: strategies used by good listeners

Metacognitive strategies

- ADVANCE ORGANISATION – before starting on a task, making a general but comprehensive preview of the concept or principle involved.
- DIRECTED ATTENTION – deciding in advance to attend in general to a learning task and to avoid irrelevant distractors (listening for 'gist').
- SELECTIVE ATTENTION – deciding in advance to attend to specific aspects of language input or situation (listening for 'cues').
- SELF-MANAGEMENT – understanding the conditions that help one learn and arranging for the presence of those conditions.
- ADVANCE PREPARATION – planning for and rehearsing the linguistic components necessary to carry out an upcoming listening task.
- SELF-MONITORING – correcting oneself for accuracy and appropriateness.
- DELAYED PRODUCTION – consciously deciding to postpone responding to a text to concentrate on understanding.
- SELF-EVALUATION – checking the outcomes of one's own language learning against an internal measure of completeness and accuracy: does it sound right? Does it make sense?

Learning to listen: strategies used by good listeners (contd)

Cognitive strategies

- REPETITION – imitating a language model, including overt practice and silent rehearsal – i.e. speaking aloud.
- RESOURCING – defining or expanding an understanding of a new word, phrase or concept through use of target-language reference materials.
- DIRECTED PHYSICAL RESPONSE – relating new information to physical actions.
- TRANSLATION – using the first language as a base for understanding the second language.
- GROUPING – reordering or reclassifying and perhaps labelling the language to be learned based on common attributes.
- NOTE-TAKING – writing down the main idea, important points, outline or summary of information presented orally.
- DEDUCTION – consciously applying rules to understand the second language.
- RECOMBINATION – constructing a meaningful sentence or larger language sequence by combining known elements in a new way.
- IMAGERY – relating new information to visual concepts in memory via familiar easily retrievable visualisations, phrases or locations.
- AUDITORY REPRESENTATION – remembering the sound of a new word, phrase or idea.
- KEY WORD – remembering a new word, phrase or idea by (1) identifying a familiar word in the first language that sounds like or otherwise resembles it, and (2) generating easily recalled images of some relationship with the new word, phrase or idea.
- CONTEXTUALISATION – placing a word or phrase in a meaningful language sequence.
- ELABORATION – relating new information to other concepts already memorised.
- TRANSFER – using previously acquired linguistic and/or conceptual knowledge to help make listening easier.
- INFERENCING – using available information to guess meanings of new items, predict outcomes, or fill in missing information.

Social/affective strategies

- CO-OPERATION – working with one or more peers to obtain feedback, pool information, or model language.
- QUESTION FOR CLARIFICATION – asking a teacher or other native speaker for repetition, paraphrasing, explanation and/or examples.

Conclusion

Evidence from research into listening and reading looking at how effective first and second language listeners listen, and how second language learners learn to listen more effectively, suggests that more effective learners are:

- more aware of what they are doing when they listen;
- use a wider range of listening strategies;
- use strategies more frequently;
- use strategies more appropriately.

This, above all, will be important when we put together a programme for our advanced learners.

key points

LISTENING INVOLVES:
- perception skills;
- analysis skills;
- synthesis skills.

WHAT MAKES LISTENING DIFFICULT OR EASY:
- the features of the text;
- the speaker;
- the nature of the task;
- the skills of the listener;
- the strategies used by the listener.

GOOD LISTENERS:
- are aware of and use appropriately a wide range of cognitive processes, e.g. decoding sound, rhythm and intonation and applying the meaning to them, interpreting subtext and transferring meaning;
- are aware of and use appropriately a wide range of metacognitive processes, e.g. focusing on gist or focusing on cues, planning ahead and evaluating progress;
- have an awareness of real-life listening as an interactive process; ask for help when needed;
- develop a degree of automaticity in using all the necessary processes and cognitive functions simultaneously.

2

The effective listener at A level – developing strategy awareness

Chapter 1 gave us a basis for understanding the skill of listening – the first step towards being able to communicate this understanding to our students. The next step, then, is to see how this understanding can be put into practice and this chapter explores how teachers can help students to develop an awareness of the strategies they will need to be effective listeners, and how they can put these strategies into practice. It looks first at the listening strategies our students bring with them from GCSE, then at what strategies they need for A level, and finally at how we can set about creating a programme of strategy awareness that will help our students develop their listening skills.

GCSE listening skills – what do our learners already know?

To gain a grade A at GCSE in MFL, our advanced students had to do the following:

- understand gist;
- identify main points in a variety of types of authentic spoken language;
- identify detail in a variety of types of authentic spoken language;
- recognise points of view, attitudes and emotions;
- draw conclusions.

A candidate at GCSE who gained a C grade could:

- identify and note main points from language spoken at normal speed;
- extract details from language spoken at normal speed;
- extract points of view from language spoken at normal speed.

All GCSE candidates encounter texts that include past and future events, drawn from a variety of topics which include familiar language in unfamiliar contexts. They practise answering a range of question types, normally requiring non-verbal or short verbal responses in the target language. The texts are of varying length, but do not require the students to remember too much at once: announcements, short conversations, instructions, short news items and telephone messages, for example, together with some longer material which, at Higher level, would have included some complex, unfamiliar language in a range of registers, together with non-factual and narrative material. The students would have been expected to understand discussion of a wide range of issues, within the scope of the GCSE topic areas, which are necessarily more limited in scope than at AS/A level.

Successful students at GCSE level will have developed a number of strategies to aid them in their listening, although they may not be explicitly aware of them:

1. ignoring words which are not needed for a successful completion of the task set;
2. using the verbal context to infer the meaning of new words;
3. making use of grammatical markers and categories, e.g. clues such as the plural forms of nouns or verbs, the ways verbs change to form tenses, word order and other such features which help them to recognise to which category (verb, noun, adjective, etc) an unknown word belongs;
4. making use of the social and cultural context;
5. using common patterns that exist between words in the foreign language, for example when case endings are added;
6. using common patterns that exist between words in English and the foreign language (i.e. cognates).

GCSE clearly requires some proficiency in listening, and teachers should not underestimate what their students already know, even if these students are not particularly aware, as in their listening in English, that they can actually use a range of strategies to listen effectively. That said, students embarking on an A level course often receive a shock when they first encounter A level type texts and tasks, partly because of the unfamiliarity of the material, partly because it all appears so much more difficult and partly – perhaps most significantly – because they do not yet know how they can improve their listening skills. The central aim of this chapter is to show teachers how students can actively develop their skills but, before we turn to the details, we should look first at what our students are aiming for.

Bridging the gap – what are students aiming for at advanced level?

The AS and A level performance descriptions give a good insight into what advanced students need to aim for in their listening skills. These skills are assessed for the most part alongside other language skills in a mixed skill approach, and are detailed in Assessment Objective 1, to 'understand and respond, in speech and writing, to spoken language'. The guidance provided in the performance description allows a clear picture to emerge of the level advanced students must reach to gain the best grades.

To obtain a **grade A/B** students need to do the following, in response to listening texts appropriate to the level, and about topics covered at that level:

AS level	A level
a show a clear understanding of spoken language;	
b understand the main points and details, including points of view, and are able to infer meaning;	
c be able to transfer meaning **with only a few omissions**;	**c** be able to transfer meaning **with only minor omissions**;
d be able to develop their ideas, and express points of view, **with some justification**;	**d** be able to develop their ideas and express and **justify points of view effectively**;
e respond readily and fluently and take the initiative *(speaking)*;	
f have generally accurate pronunciation and intonation *(speaking)*;	
g be able to deal with unpredictable elements *(speaking)*;	
h show the ability to organise and structure their response coherently *(writing)*;	
i offer relevant information which addresses the requirements of the task *(writing)*.	

To give some indication of the boundary for a pass grade at AS and A level, the following performance descriptions reflect performance at **E/U grades**. Students working at these levels will do the following in their listening, again in response to listening texts appropriate to the level, and about topics covered at that level:

AS level	A level
a show some understanding of spoken language, but may experience difficulties with more complex language;	
b understand some of the main points and details, including points of view and have a limited ability to infer meaning, where appropriate to the task;	
c be able to convey **some** basic information when transferring meaning;	**c** be able to convey **the basic information** when transferring meaning;
d may be hesitant in their response and their fluency is often confined to pre-learnt material;	
e their target-language performance may be influenced by their first language *(speaking)*;	
f may have some difficulty communicating factual information, narrating events and expressing points of view in response to the task set, and do not always address the requirements of the task *(writing)*;	
g show some ability to structure and organise their response, where appropriate.	

The list of descriptors provides a comprehensive list of required skills and an important focus for students. It is worth noting – and this comparison brings it out very clearly – that the aspects of performance assessed at both AS and A2 are the same, and the difference in the levels is achieved by the greater linguistic and cultural demands of the text input. The gradations between the grade descriptions are achieved by a fine-tuning in the choice of descriptive terminology, between for example 'clear understanding' and 'some understanding', and between 'able to infer meaning' and 'have a limited ability to infer meaning'.

Strategies for improving listening

Clearly, students will want to aim for the highest level of proficiency that they can achieve. The A level performance descriptions are an 'endpoint' – what students need to achieve by the end of their advanced level studies. In order to reach this stage, and to reach the levels demanded, we need to encourage our students to employ a range of strategies. This is where O'Malley and Chamot's list of strategies from the end of Chapter 1 to help students to listen more effectively comes into its own. It provides us with a very appropriate range of advanced listening strategies which good listeners at advanced level can usefully use to improve their skills.

Perhaps the most important aspect of listening to emerge from the evidence in Chapter 1 is that, for a listener to be effective, he/she must learn to develop the cognitive processes necessary for effective listening, which means that he/she must learn to use a wide variety of strategies. Cognitive strategies help learners to decode and remember meaning; social/affective strategies help them to ask for help and learn from one another, and metacognitive strategies help them to plan their listening and how they will improve how they listen. What the identification of all these strategies reminds us is that when students are learning how to listen, listening tasks do not always have to take the form of tests – listening texts can be used in all sorts of different ways, with the learner encouraged to focus on one or more of the different strategies, with a view to improving the strategy involved in understanding. A teacher can explain the meaning of a listening text; only a student can practise the strategies needed to understand it for him or herself.

What follows, then, is an expanded list of the strategies drawn together after research (see Chapter 1), with ideas for their practical application. The goal of the teacher is to draw his or her students' attention to these as strategies for making their listening more effective, and for improving their listening, in the hope that they will adopt them and use them. Some of the strategies appear contradictory and certainly cannot be practised together. Students should not feel concerned about this – what is important is that they learn what the different strategies involve so that they can make an informed choice about which to use and when, depending on the task and their preferences. Not all students will like all the strategies! The aim, of course, is for this choice of strategies to become so well established with students that they are able to select almost automatically the best way to listen to the text and task ahead of them.

How to use the strategies: ideas for teachers

The sections that follow contain:

- eight metacognitive strategies:
  - advance organisation;
  - directed attention;
  - selective attention;

- self-management;
- advance preparation;
- self-monitoring;
- delayed production;
- self-evaluation.

■ fifteen cognitive strategies:
- repetition;
- resourcing;
- directed physical response;
- translation;
- grouping;
- note-taking;
- deduction;
- recombination;
- imagery;
- auditory representation;
- key word;
- contextualisation;
- elaboration;
- transfer;
- inferencing.

■ two social/affective strategies:
- co-operation;
- question for clarification.

The strategies are not given in any particular order of difficulty, as such an order does not exist universally for every student, and they will all fit into the advice given in the section immediately following the lists about raising strategy awareness. Teachers will want to read through the list, perhaps focusing on specific strategies which they know their learners find difficult, and highlighting them for practice. Alternatively, teachers may wish to draw out all the strategies that they know their learners can do well, to help them see what successful listening involves. Teachers can certainly encourage students to try out the strategies one at a time – not necessarily in order – guiding them by their choice of text and task (see Chapter 3). The strategies are presented here in a photocopiable format aimed at students, with ideas about how to use them so that they can start thinking about which strategies suit their learning styles, the listening tasks which they encounter and the type of text which they will have to tackle in their advanced level course.

3 Metacognitive strategies

S

Strategy	**Advance organisation**
Description	Predicting or previewing the likely content of a listening activity.
Applications	• Practise reading the questions beforehand to predict the content of the listening text, including the issues likely to be raised, any stance taken, etc. • Work out in advance what kind of text it is – a conversation? A news report? Knowing what to expect will make it easier to understand the text, because you will be able to draw on your expectations of the format as well as the content – the type of language used, for instance.

Strategy	**Directed attention**
Description	Deciding in advance to listen for the main points in a text and to avoid irrelevant distractors (listening for 'gist').
Applications	• Do not prepare thoroughly before listening – just listen and glean as much information from the text as possible. • Practise listening out for the key points in a text from 'cold' – just listen and then review what you have understood. If you practise this strategy a lot, you will develop a confidence in listening to the unexpected.

Strategy	**Selective attention**
Description	Deciding in advance to attend to specific aspects of language input or situation (listening for 'cues').
Applications	• Ask yourself what the questions are asking for and think carefully about what sorts of responses you might expect to find in the text (don't make up your mind in advance about answers, though!). Listen out for this sort of language in the text to help you decide where the answers lie. • If you are listening without any questions to help prompt you, try to guess what words, phrases and ideas you might encounter. Make a list of them and as you listen, cross them off.

checklist

3

S

Metacognitive strategies (contd)

Strategy   **Self-management**

Description   Understanding your own learning processes and making sure you apply those processes to a task.

Applications
- Find out about your learning preferences – what kind of a learner are you? (linguistic, visual, etc?).
- Use this information to help you decide the best way for you to learn to listen more effectively – which strategies will suit your learning style best?
- Experiment with listening at different times of the day and in different situations (at home, at school/college, etc) – which suits you best? When and where do you feel your listening is most successful? Focus on these times and places for the future!

Strategy   **Advance preparation**

Description   Planning for and rehearsing the language items necessary to carry out an upcoming listening task.

Applications
- Look at the listening task and guess what the topic will focus on.
- Look again at all the materials you covered when you came across this topic for the first time, especially vocabulary and key phrases and spend some time learning them before you listen.
- What other vocabulary do you think you might need before you listen? Look it up in a dictionary or consult a topic-based vocabulary resource.
- Listen out for these words and phrases when you listen as they will help you understand what is going on. You will have been most successful in your preparation if you recognise all the topic-specific words and phrases in the text!

3

S

Metacognitive strategies (contd)

Strategy	**Self-monitoring**
Description	Correcting oneself for accuracy and appropriateness.
Applications	• As you listen, scribble notes on what you hear, trying to be as accurate as possible (but instantly). After each time you listen, check what you have written – does it make sense? Have you written any nonsense words? Try to correct what you have written and listen again. Finally, check with a transcript if you can.

Strategy	**Delayed production**
Description	Consciously deciding to postpone responding to a text to concentrate on understanding.
Applications	• Don't worry about answering the questions – you can read them and be aware of them, but the most important point of this strategy is to understand everything you hear. • Listen again and again to the text until you feel confident that you understand it – use various other strategies to help you (including looking up words in the dictionary etc). • Use the transcript to help you understand the text.

Strategy	**Self-evaluation**
Description	Checking the outcomes of one's own language learning against a personal checklist of completeness and accuracy.
Applications	• Check with yourself before you answer any questions – does what you want to say make sense? Does the passage itself make sense? If not, there is still something you haven't quite understood. • Keep a record of what you listen to and how you feel about the tasks (e.g. using Resource Sheet 5, p41, as a template). Do you feel you are getting better? • Keep vocabulary lists from each of the texts you listen to and review them regularly. Do you now know all the words on the lists and can you reproduce them accurately?

checklist

4

S

Cognitive strategies

| Strategy | Repetition |

| Description | Imitating a language model, including speaking aloud and silent rehearsal. |

| Applications | • Practise saying what you hear, repeating again and again until you feel that you are saying it how you hear it. You may find a transcript and a tape recorder useful for this. You will also improve your speaking skills, but above all you will gain an understanding of how the word or phrase will sound next time you hear it, and you will find it easier to identify. |

| Strategy | Resourcing |

| Description | Defining or expanding an understanding of a new word, phrase or concept through use of target-language reference materials. |

| Applications | • Listen carefully to the context of the words that are new – can you work out what kind of a word it is (verb, noun, etc) and what it might mean? Learning to listen to the immediate context can help fix sounds and meanings in your mind for the next time you hear them.
• You can also look up words you don't understand in a target-language dictionary to learn them in context. |

| Strategy | Directed physical response |

| Description | Relating new information to physical actions. |

| Applications | • Make listening an active task – walk around as you listen and pretend you are speaking too – declaim, make gestures and emphasise the words and phrases you hear.
• Listen again and again and practise your actions until you can practically do without the text. |

Cognitive strategies (contd)

S

| **Strategy** | **Translation** |

| **Description** | Using the first language as a base for understanding the second language. |

| **Applications** | • Note down words you hear but do not understand and use a dictionary to find out what they mean. |

• Listen out for cognates and words that are similar in English. You may not always be right about their meaning, so do check them carefully in a dictionary too.

• NB you may find a transcript useful here if you are having difficulty identifying some of the words you need to look up, but do not rely on it immediately – practise listening out for words and guessing what they will look like.

| **Strategy** | **Grouping** |

| **Description** | Reordering or reclassifying and perhaps labelling the new language based on common attributes. |

| **Applications** | • Once you have listened to the text and found out what the new words and phrases were which you did not understand, make a note of them in groups according to meaning (topic areas), frequency (most common to least common) and/or appropriateness for certain formats (the phrases most likely to be heard in a television news broadcast, for instance). You can do this on paper or on separate cassettes – the latter has many advantages for prompting recall, as long as you have recorded the words and phrases accurately and at a typical speed, but can be cumbersome to organise. A personal stereo or a dictaphone and set of mini-cassettes come into their own here, however. |

checklist

Cognitive strategies (contd)

Strategy Note-taking

Description Writing down the main idea, important points, outline or summary of information presented orally.

Applications
- NB you may find it helpful to use this strategy in conjunction with one or more of the meta-cognitive strategies described above (e.g. delayed production, advanced organisation).
- As you listen, try to write down what you hear – not every word, but the main points. You can do this with or without a template depending on your preferences and whether or not you need help to be able to identify clearly the structure of what you are listening to. A simple template (e.g. with the headings 'what?' 'where?' 'who?' etc) might be useful in the early stages.

Strategy Deduction

Description Consciously applying rules to understand the second language.

Applications
- If you don't understand something when listening, try to narrow down what kind of a word it is and then think about the sound rules you have come across to help you work out what the word might be – remember silent consonants, for example.
- Think – could the set of sounds you are hearing be more than one word? Try to work out from the intonation and the individual sounds where the likely breaks are.
- Try using the occasional listening text as a dictation exercise, writing down every single word. This is a rigorous exercise, and it certainly stretches your deductive powers!

Strategy	Recombination
Description	Constructing a meaningful sentence or larger language sequence by combining known elements in a new way.
Applications	• Once you have identified new words, don't just remember them in their immediate context. Think of other phrases, sentences and texts in which they might appear and make something up to help you remember them in a new context. Don't forget to say them aloud or record them!

Strategy	Imagery
Description	Relating new information to visual concepts in memory via familiar easily retrievable visualisations, phrases or locations.
Applications	• As you listen, try to imagine what you can hear – imagine the people speaking, or imagine what is being talked about. This will help create an image in your mind which will fix the word and its meaning more effectively.

Strategy	Auditory representation
Description	Remembering the sound of a new word, phrase or idea.
Applications	• Record vocabulary on a tape and play it repeatedly. • When you are practising vocabulary, read it aloud and listen to yourself speaking.

checklist

Cognitive strategies (contd)

Strategy | **Key word**

Description

Remembering a new word, phrase or idea by (1) identifying a familiar word in the first language that sounds like or otherwise resembles it, and (2) generating easily recalled images of some relationship with the new word, phrase or idea.

Applications

- There are many ways you can employ this strategy – mnemonics, for instance, or word association, which you may have come across in study and revision skills training. The most important thing to remember is that you are not just interested in how a word appears, but in how it sounds, and particularly how it sounds when spoken in real life. Make sure you say things aloud while learning too!

Strategy | **Contextualisation**

Description

Placing a word or phrase in a meaningful language sequence.

Applications

- Try to remember the new words and phrases you encounter in the context of the original text where you heard them. Keep listening texts and exercises in the same way that you keep reading texts, with words highlighted and easily seen when you glance back through your notes.

- You can also write down or record any new words you encounter in a sentence form – this may help you to remember them when you hear them again.

Cognitive strategies (contd)

Strategy	Elaboration

Description	Relating new information to other concepts already memorised.

Applications	• When you listen to something new, make sure that you write it down with words of a similar nature or connected with the same topic. If – each time you add to this sort of list – you read all the words out aloud, you will create a joint association of meaning and sound which will help you to remember them when you hear one of them in the future.

Strategy	Transfer

Description	Using previously acquired language and/or concepts to help make listening easier.

Applications	• When you listen, relax – let the words wash over you and ask yourself – what do they remind me of? If you can allow your brain to draw out itself all the words, phrases and ideas that it can find that are similar to the ones you are hearing, you will soon start to make connections!

Strategy	Inferencing

Description	Using available information to guess meanings of new items, predict outcomes, or fill in missing information.

Applications	• As you listen, try to guess what some words or phrases or sections might be about, bearing in mind what the rest is about. Focus on difficult sections and listen again and again so that you can narrow down the phrases you don't understand to manageable proportions. Guess – and check afterwards!

checklist

5 S

Social/affective strategies

Strategy | Co-operation

Description | Work with one or more peers to obtain feedback, pool information, or model language.

Applications |
- Listen with a partner or friend and talk about what you hear. You will probably understand slightly different bits of the text in slightly different ways and by sharing your understandings you will each be able to piece together a better picture. This strategy can help you see how other people think as they are listening, particularly if you think aloud in discussion, and this may give you some useful pointers for the future.

Strategy | Question for clarification

Description | Ask a teacher or other native speaker for repetition, paraphrasing, explanation and/or examples.

Applications |
- When you are listening in class, ask when you don't understand. Try not to ask for the answer in English – instead, see if your teacher or Foreign Language Assistant can give you some explanation in the foreign language which will help you to make sense of what you have heard. Go back to the text and listen again – does it make more sense now?

checklist

Strategy awareness and training in practice: an example

For strategy practice to be effective, it needs to be part of an overall plan, a programme where teachers are able to feel confident that they are exposing their students to the right sorts of materials and tasks to help them to become more confident in the use of a range of strategies for improved listening. We will look in Chapter 3 at the choice of texts and tasks, and how to audit existing listening materials to see how useful they are in allowing students to become aware of the strategies they might want to use. In this section, however, we look at the framework for a strategic awareness programme. Essentially, we need to find a way for these strategies to become part of our teaching, and teachers may find the following approach helpful:

1. raising awareness in students – helping them to see first that there is a need for them to use strategies in listening, and secondly what those strategies can be;
2. selection of appropriate texts and tasks and organising practice (dealt with in Chapter 3);
3. evaluation and self-evaluation – crucial for teachers and students to measure progress and prepare the ground for further strategy use.

We will look at areas 1 and 3 now, with practical ideas to stimulate student discussion and openness to learning.

Raising awareness

The first thing that teachers need to do in any programme designed to improve strategic competence is to find a way to begin to make students aware of the processes that they are using in listening. The resource sheets here and in Appendix 1 (see p91) may be useful as a starting point. Resource Sheet 1 opposite is a series of prompts for discussion and can be used on the overhead projector or in group work or pairwork to stimulate ideas and discussion about what makes a good (and a better) listener. For this discussion you should be able to draw on many of the strategies identified at the end of Chapter 1 and expanded earlier in this chapter. Your goal is to let the students discover for themselves as many listening strategies as possible, but you may find that a back-up sheet with the list of strategies and a short description (e.g. Checklist 2 on pp17–18), which you can produce at the end of the discussion, is a useful summary for students.

Prompts for discussion

What skills will I need for the exam?

What kinds of texts do I need to listen to?

What do I need to do before, during and after listening?

What does good listening involve?

What will make me a good listener at A level?

How often should I do some listening?

What is easy and what is difficult about listening in a foreign language?

How can I tell if I am improving?

What resources are available for me to use?

How good am I at listening?

What do I need to do to help myself get better?

- ....
- ....
- ....
- ....

resource sheet

Alternatively, Resource sheet 2 (see Appendix 1, p91) – a questionnaire designed to focus students on their current level of strategic competence in listening – may be helpful. The purpose of both of these resource sheets is to introduce students to a range of strategies for effective listening that they may not have encountered. Students need to be receptive to the idea of strategy development if it is to have any chance of success, and these resource sheets will sow the seeds of awareness before the students can begin the process of actively developing the strategies that they already use, as well as other strategies that may be new to them or that they have yet to develop to their full extent.

Resource sheet 3 takes these initial discussions a step further and is an example of what you should be able to draw up after such a class discussion – a concrete list of how students should approach their listening in order to develop their skills, and this can be used in conjunction with the list of strategies on pp17–18. If the best way for students to learn to listen more effectively is for them to take responsibility for their own listening, they need as much access as possible to what we know about listening and, equally, they need to have ownership of this information. If a personalised sheet similar to this one can emerge from their own discussions, supplemented by the thoughts and experiences of others, including the teacher, then it is far more likely that the advice it contains will be heeded.

Evaluating skills

Depending on how receptive your students are to the idea that they possess and use certain strategies when they listen – strategies which they can work to improve – you may find that you can combine at an early stage stimulating awareness of strategies for improving listening with an evaluation or self-evaluation of the skills the students actually use. A helpful resource for this is Resource sheet 4 (p40), which encourages students to pick a minimum of two listening texts – the Internet is a good source (see p59) – and to assess how effectively they listen and what they do when they listen. To encourage students to develop a sense of ownership of the listening strategies they will use and to begin to take on responsibility for developing them, it is a good idea to ask your students to choose texts that are of particular interest to them – about recent stories, fashion or hobbies. The tasks in Resource Sheet 4, once completed, should form the focus of a discussion either with peers or with the teacher, to draw the attention of the students to what they do and what they could do better. As before, you need to be prepared to produce a list of potential strategies and to guide students in their usage – the students will look to the teacher to expand their understanding and will need access to information about the wide range of strategies available, as well as needing to discuss how they might consider using them.

3

S

How to improve listening strategies

Below are some strategies you might use when you listen. Ask yourself ...

- what do they involve you doing?
- do you use them?
- when do you already use them?
- when might you consider using them?

Strategies to help me comprehend a text

Depending on what the task is, I could ...

- try to predict from the context what will come up – ideas, vocabulary, etc;
- listen to the tone the speakers are using;
- not worry if I can't hear or understand a word – it may not matter;
- avoid concentrating on individual words at the expense of understanding the whole;
- read the questions first so I can listen for specific information;
- listen for key words such as main verbs and subjects – words that are essential to understanding the meaning of the text;
- try to combine the words I hear with a sensible understanding of the topic BUT don't make up what I haven't heard!
- try to work out the meanings of words from the context – use words that are similar words in the foreign language or in English as clues;
- double-check my answers – if they don't make sense, they can't be right!
- listen out for linking words.

Opportunities to help me practise and improve my performance

- go to a country where the foreign language is spoken;
- speak to the Foreign Language Assistant;
- listen to the radio in the foreign language;
- listen to the radio on-line;
- watch satellite television news;
- get used to hearing lots of different types of texts;
- make my vocabulary knowledge more active;
- practise a lot!

resource sheet

4

S

Evaluating listening skills

Ecouter, ça fait plaisir!

Tâche 1:

1. Choisis un texte **qui t'intéresse** – n'importe quel texte – sur Internet (de deux minutes). Quel est le titre du texte et où est-ce qu'il se trouve?
2. Ecoute le texte au minimum deux fois.
3. Combien as-tu compris, à peu près?

   rien ▬▬▬▬▬▬▬▬▬▬▬▬▬▬▬▬▬▬▬▬▬▬ tout

4. De quoi s'agit-il dans le texte?

Tâche 2:

1. Choisis un texte sur Internet (de deux minutes) qui t'intéresse. Cette fois, le texte doit avoir comme sujet un aspect **que tu trouves assez ennuyeux**. Quel est le titre du texte et où est-ce qu'il se trouve?
2. Ecoute le texte au minimum deux fois.
3. Combien as-tu compris, à peu près?

   rien ▬▬▬▬▬▬▬▬▬▬▬▬▬▬▬▬▬▬▬▬▬▬ tout

4. De quoi s'agit-il dans le texte?

To think about and note down on the other side of this sheet:
- which listening skills do you think you have practised in these exercises?
- why is listening so important to your understanding of French?
- how do you think you can improve your listening?

The main premise of any programme to encourage the development of listening skills at advanced levels is that the students need to be guided into an awareness both of what they already do when they listen and how they could do it better. Armed with this information, they need to be exposed to a number of listening texts and tasks and this will be looked at more closely in Chapter 3. As a prelude to the discussion, however, if students are encouraged to keep notes of what they listen to, what they are listening for, which strategies they are using, and how effective they feel they are becoming as listeners, they can evaluate their own skills with every listening task in which they engage. This can be tracked by teachers and students for each topic or theme followed in class quite simply using Resource Sheet 5.

5

S

Tracking progress

TOPIC: ....

Tasks (what I had to do/page no, etc)	Mark or comment	How easy did I find it?	What listening strategies did I use in this task?	Am I getting better at using these strategies?	What can I do to be even better next time?
1.					
2.					
3.					
4.					
5.					
6.					

- How have my listening skills improved in this topic?
- What do I still need to work on?
- How can I do this?

resource sheet

The following is a broad outline of a programme to develop strategic awareness in listening skills, based on experience. It is an example of how strategies can be incorporated into everyday teaching at advanced level.

Case study

Advanced level listening – strategy development
Simon Green, Language Teaching Adviser, CILT, the National Centre for Languages

----

Listening to a substantial amount of text without attention to a clear set of strategies is a challenging task for anyone at any level of language learning, but particularly so at advanced level. What I have found works well with students is a gentler introduction to listening to a text via a process of sensitisation to the language.

The pattern is:

- anticipate;
- suggest;
- feedback;
- sensitise;
- listen for language;
- feedback;
- comprehension.

Anticipate

Before listening to any text in the target language, it is helpful to invite the students to suggest any vocabulary or phrases that they would anticipate hearing on any given topic.

If we take a news broadcast, for example, we could ask: 'What do you think would be the key headlines in the target language country this morning?' – politics/events/crime/sport/business, etc. Students should work with a partner on this for a few minutes and try to say as much as possible in the target language.

Suggest

Students then make suggestions in the target language about the kind of language that they think they will hear when they first listen to the broadcast. Encourage them to be as precise as possible about the vocabulary and phrases.

As they make suggestions, write these on the board and listen out for what they are not saying. If they are merely presenting a list of nouns, encourage them to come up with some verbs, verbal phrases, or even sentences.

Feedback

After students have made their suggestions, provide some extra comments to the students about the language they have selected.

- How did you arrive at that reply?
- Did you actually hear the news or are you speculating?
- Is there another way we could express this in the target language?

All the time, try to encourage them to experiment with the language that they already know and to anticipate not only the linguistic content of the text but also the cultural references. This can be further helped by feeding in some of the phrases that will come up.

Sensitise

During the first hearing of the text, the students may well not understand much of the content. So, ask them simply to listen out for the vocabulary and phrases that have been discussed and note whether they come up in the broadcast. This sensitising of the ear to the first listening is crucial. Much of the broadcast may be difficult to pick up on the first hearing, but by focusing on specific vocabulary and phrases they are on the alert and should find it easier to note such language from their own suggestions.

Listen for language

After listening to the text for the first time, select five or six categories of language that you want your students to listen out for: for example, in French, words ending in -ion(s), any adjectives, any named places, any numbers and times, and one phrase which requires them to add only the following word.

Play the recording and watch the students as they write down the words they have heard. Their body language alone will tell you if they have coped with the task. When the recording has finished, invite the students to feedback each of the categories and write them on the board under separate headings.

The following example (p44) of a news bulletin in French is followed by suggested categories that students could be asked to listen out for.

– Vous écoutez Radio-Service Compris. Il est 11h30 et c'est l'heure de retrouver Philippe Roussel, pour un flash d'informations.

– Bonjour. Les grands titres du journal de 14 heures.

Tout d'abord, la circulation. Il y a des embouteillages sur toutes les routes en direction des sports d'hiver! On me signale un bouchon de 25 kilomètres près de Grenoble et aussi un important ralentissement dû à un accident, à la sortie de Toulouse. Des précisions à 14 heures avec notre specialiste de la route, Laurent Brunetot.

Un hold-up tragique a eu lieu ce matin dans une banque du boulevard Saint-Michel, à Paris. Les malfaiteurs ont pénétré dans l'agence de la BNP un peu après l'ouverture. Ils étaient armés. Un employé de la banque a réussi à alerter la police.

Malheureusement, les malfaiteurs ont pris peur et ont tiré plusieurs coups de feu. Bilan: un mort et cinq blessés. La police n'a pas encore retrouvé les gangsters. Plus de détails et l'interview de quelques témoins à 14 heures.

(from: *Radio Service Compris* – Mary Glasgow Publications)

Here is an example of five categories that students could be asked to listen out for:

Numbers/ times	Named places and people	Adjectives	les malfaiteurs ont +	Words ending in ...-ion(s)
11h30	Grenoble	grands	pénétré	informations
14	Paris	toutes	pris peur	circulation
25	Philippe Roussel	important		direction
un	Laurence Brunetot	tragique		précisions
cinq		armés		
		quelques		

For the purposes of differentiation, give more able students categories such as named places or adjectives, as they need to be able to recognise and understand the text at speed to do the task. Give the other students the 'trigger cues' such as *les malfaiteurs ont* + because all they have to do is listen out for that trigger word and write down the word that follows.

They could then construct new sentences based on what they have heard, for example:

A 11h30 Philippe Roussel a pénétré dans une banque à Paris.

Feedback

Following the above exercise, provide every student with the transcript of the text they have been listening to.

Play the recording again from the beginning and ask students to follow the transcript as they **listen** to the target language. Tell them that after a short while you will turn down the sound but they must continue to read along in their heads at the same speed as they think the original would run. Then press 'pause' and tell them to stop. The students must then underline the word that they think they will hear next when you release the pause button. Turn up the sound while the pause button is down. Students then compare and feedback the word that they think they will hear next. You write these suggestions on the board and then, very deliberately, play the next word.

Comprehension

During these listening exercises, the students have been concentrating solely on the language – the vocabulary and structures. At no point have they been asked the meaning of the passage they have heard. They will now be quite familiar with the text, having heard it several times and the next task is to prepare a series of comprehension questions based on the text. For this they will need resources such as a dictionary and they will need a framework to fit the questions in. At this point they will need to process the text like a teacher and, in the processing, they will learn a fair amount of vocabulary.

They can also prepare a mark scheme and some of their suggestions could be tried out with a parallel group.

Conclusion

Listening to a disembodied voice in the target language is a difficult task. If it can be made a little more accessible by judicious use of some of the methods suggested above, it goes a long way to helping students grasp one of the essential skills of learning a language at an advanced level.

The key benefits of following the pattern suggested may be summarised as:

- increased motivation;
- increased awareness of language forms and structures;
- better understanding of sound-spelling links;
- better appreciation of rhythms of language;
- accessibility to the language in spoken form;
- greater challenge to understand the meaning after an appreciation of the form.

How effective is strategy training?

This case study shows in practice how we can find a way to train our students to develop the listening skills they need, built into a programme or around our existing scheme of work. Can we be sure, however, that the teaching of strategic competence is effective? O'Malley (1987: 143), who conducted research into the teachability of strategic competence, concludes:

> *Teachers should be confident that there exist a number of strategies which can be embedded into their existing curricula, that can be taught to students with only modest extra effort, and that can improve the overall class performance.*

Other research, for example Tang and Moore's (1992) research into the introduction of readers to pre-reading cognitive and metacognitive strategies, shows an improvement in ability after learners are exposed to the strategy training, and, significantly (in the case, notably, of the metacognitive strategies to which the readers were introduced), the continued use of the strategies in later tasks. The readers had clearly learned and decided to continue using these strategies. Hattie et al (1996), in a review of fifty-one studies of programmes that involved active intervention in the teaching of learning skills, concluded that this teaching was effective when it followed a number of basic ground rules. The key words are 'situated cognition' (Hattie et al 1996: 99), meaning that any learner training needs to be in context and must be relevant.

Hattie et al (1990) also look at the affective factor in learning – how learners feel about what they are doing – and conclude from their analysis of the research that learner training only works if it focuses on what learners are already able to do and allows them to develop strategies from an acknowledged base of strategic competence. In other words, telling learners that they do not have the strategies they should possess, or that they are using the 'wrong' strategies, will not encourage them to develop other strategies, as Wenden (1987) discovered in her first attempt at learner training. In fact, the learners she investigated were extremely resistant to being asked to change how they learned, however ineffective the outcome may have seemed to an observer. Hattie et al (1996: 131) conclude that:

> *Strategy training should be seen as a balanced system in which the individual's abilities, insights and sense of responsibility are brought into use so that the strategies that are appropriate to the task at hand can be used.*

- Strategic competence in listening can and should be taught, and teachers need to encourage students to develop their use of a wide range of listening strategies.

- Students need to become aware of strategies they use and strategies they might adopt to become better listeners, and they should practise and develop them.

- A programme to help advanced learners improve their listening should include the following steps:
  1. raising awareness in students;
  2. selection of appropriate texts and tasks and practice;
  3. evaluation and self-evaluation.

- Learner training only works if it focuses on what learners are already able to do and allows them to develop strategies from an acknowledged base of strategic competence.

3

Improving listening skills – developing a scheme of work

The context of listening strategy training: texts and tasks

Listening strategy training cannot, of course, be done in isolation – it needs appropriate texts and appropriate tasks to allow students to develop their skills. These texts and tasks can usefully follow examination type texts and tasks, although if effective listening is our goal, then we need to teach our students to use the wide range of 'environmental clues' that exist, as described in Chapter 1. In fact, in a programme to develop listening strategies, as wide a range of listening texts should be used as possible, and we should have at our disposal a wide range of tasks that we might potentially ask our students to do in order to focus their attention on the content of the texts and/or on the strategies required to understand the texts effectively. The following lists give an indication of the variety that we might want our listeners to encounter:

Types of text

- Conversations – face-to-face, recorded, or on the phone:
  - short and transactional (e.g. at the supermarket);
  - formulaic – discussing health, weekend activities, holidays etc;
  - complex – political opinions, thoughts on current affairs, philosophical discussions.

- Narratives and descriptions:
  - storytelling – audio books, children's literature;
  - relating events.

- Multimedia:
  - adverts;
  - songs;

- news;
- weather;
- TV series;
- films.

- Academic and formal:
  - interviews;
  - lectures;
  - speeches;
  - events.

Types of task – practical examples

These examples tie in with the metacognitive, cognitive and social/affective strategies explored in Chapters 1 and 2 – the strategies that help students to focus in advance on what they are likely to hear, for example, or help them to learn better listening habits through repetition and asking questions. Whereas the focus until now has been on individual student motivation – what the students can do by themselves to improve their listening, these strategies can just as effectively be encouraged by teachers, and by choosing to set types of task which will demand certain strategies in response, teachers can in a very practical way help encourage their students to become better listeners.

Pre-listening tasks

- anticipating or predicting what will be said from related stimulus material;
- brainstorming vocabulary and ideas.

During listening tasks

- compare what is heard with a list of ideas/phrases/words provided by the teacher in advance;
- answer true/false to a series of pre-prepared statements;
- fill in the gaps in a short transcript or summary;
- identify synonyms or antonyms of key words and phrases;
- use part or all of the text for a dictation exercise;
- interpret (simultaneously or with some delay) for someone who does not understand the language (see Appendix 2 for a case study of interpreting in practice in the classroom, p95).

Post-listening tasks

- check comprehension by comparing notes and seeking clarification from others;
- record – in writing or on tape – useful phrases and constructions;
- prepare an oral or written summary of the text for an outsider;
- produce a similar text – e.g. an advert or interview;
- prepare for a debate based on the topic of the text and using the ideas and language encountered.

Choosing texts and choosing tasks – pitching it right

The above types of text and task contain a wide variety of levels of difficulty, and an important part of the teacher's role is to select texts and tasks appropriate to the needs of the students. No two programmes to develop listening skills in advanced learners will have the same content. Much will depend on the learners themselves – how advanced they are, what they and you feel they should be doing to improve, what topic areas they need to work on to build up the background knowledge necessary for successful listening, and how much support they need in the process. Different learners have different needs – and will find different types of text more or less difficult. After all, as Rost (1990: 159) says, 'text difficulty relates to affective factors of learner interest and motivation' as much as to a notional idea of perceived difficulty, which is in itself very difficult to determine, as examiners will testify! The task of selecting texts and encouraging strategy use is one that very much depends on the experience of the teacher and how well he/she knows the students. Of course, the teacher must always remember that the text the learners hear has to stretch them to some extent, as it is only by being asked to do something a little beyond their existing capabilities that they will actively develop their cognitive processes.

The following checklist for assessing the level of complexity of a text, then, provides only a guideline for teachers who would like to gather texts for use in a graded programme. Although its primary use is to help teachers to select texts, teachers may also find it helpful to show to their students and let them try it out, in order to let them see how different factors affect how easy or difficult a text is to understand. This can help students to feel they are able to approach apparently complex tasks with more confidence, and an awareness of text difficulty will also allow students to be more prepared to deal with the challenge ahead of them. The checklist covers the source of the text, the number and type of speakers, and the content – the medium and the message. Again, different learners will find different types of text more or less difficult, especially as they will have more or less of an understanding of different topic areas approached in the text. The checklist does, however, allow teachers to compare different texts and thereby to ensure that their students are exposed to an appropriate variety in the course of a programme to improve their listening.

Assessing the simplicity of a text

1. Source of text:

   - authentic (originally intended for a native speaker of the language)
   - pedagogic (edited and simplified for teaching purposes)

2. Speaker(s)

   - authentic one or more
     - monologue
     - dialogue
     - conversation
     - discussion
     - interview
   - gender – all male or all female voices
   - register (formality – informality – colloquiality)
   - accent
   - speed of delivery

3. Content

   - medium
     - vocabulary
     - structural range
   - message
     - factual
     - abstract
     - explicitly stated
     - implicit – to be inferred
     - organisation (sequential, as in a scripted or formal format, or more haphazard, as in conversation)

© CILT, the National Centre for Languages 2004

This variety of text is important so that students can be exposed to breadth in their practice – quality and quantity, in fact. Equally important in any kind of strategy training programme, however, is the type of task set. If students are actively employing some of the metacognitive strategies suggested earlier, then strictly speaking it will not always be necessary to set tasks to accompany texts, but most students find it difficult to work without a focus and benefit from direction when listening. If teachers remind students to use these strategies (and give them an indication of which ones they will find most helpful), it is likely to prove extremely beneficial to the students. Both for reasons of student support and in order to retain some control over the process of strategy development, teachers will often, if not usually, wish to set tasks to accompany listening texts. This will ensure that a wide range of strategies is used by the students, and that they do not become disheartened by trying to do too much at once – and failing. The checklist below puts task types in a rough order, from less difficult to more difficult, so that teachers can take this into account as well as the text difficulty when they assess what they are asking their learners to do. Again, it also ensures that there is scope over the course of the programme for all the necessary strategies for successful listening at advanced level to be stimulated and practised.

7 TS   Assessing the simplicity of a task

recognising information

■

noting facts

■

noting gist

■

noting opinions

■

tasks that require a high memory load

■

interpreting

■

inferring

(Adapted from Turner, 1995)

Auditing the materials to hand

Teachers can usefully audit the range of listening material they provide for their students by filling in the following grid for each topic they teach. First, a judgement needs to be made about the difficulty of the text, taking into account the features listed in Checklist 6 on p51, and the corresponding needs of the students. If a listening exercise is judged, for example, to have a difficult text but an easy task, then a tick will go in the appropriate box. Although not all boxes will necessarily be ticked for each topic, by the end of the course a general pattern should emerge that suggests full coverage (not forgetting the texts that students may have listened to independently – these too need to be written down); if the coverage is less than full, or rather biased towards one or more levels of text and task, then teachers will need to look at how they can extend what they do and explore different sources of text and task.

6
T

resource sheet

Auditing texts

Level of text difficulty	easy	medium	difficult
recognising information			
noting facts			
noting gist			
noting opinions			
tasks requiring a high memory load			
interpreting			
inferring			

© CILT, the National Centre for Languages 2004

Sourcing and exploiting advanced level listening material

There are many, many sources of good authentic material for advanced level listening and some of them are listed in Appendices 3 and 4. These fall into two main categories – 'ready-made' materials consisting of cassettes and videos, often accompanying coursebooks, and 'raw' materials, available in abundance on satellite and Internet, and these are all discussed below.

Using coursebook materials and commercial resources

'Ready-made' materials have the advantage that texts have been pre-selected to ensure that they match the requirements of advanced level courses, both in appropriate content, text difficulty and task difficulty: most 'ready-made' materials have accompanying exercises. A good starting point for advanced level listening material is the coursebook used in class, as this will ensure – as long as the coursebook is up-to-date – that listening texts are relevant to the topics to be covered in the subject specifications and in which the students are expected to develop background knowledge. This advice comes with a warning, however – make sure that you audit the texts carefully using the checklists above before relying on them solely as a source of texts for a programme designed to develop strategy awareness. In many cases there are not enough listening texts of a sufficiently varied nature in content, type of task and range of voice and speaker, to be able to provide the basis for good exposure. Moreover, if students are limited to the coursebook, they will not learn to explore the variety of texts available to them to help them take on some responsibility for their own learning themselves.

Of particular interest are the 'stand-alone' cassette and video resources, including resources such as *Authentik*, published regularly to accompany a magazine or newspaper and specifically designed for advanced level study – they too come complete with transcripts and sets of exercises which can make planning and preparation on the part of the teacher much more straightforward, and, compared to a coursebook, they are less constrained by the demands of space and strict relevance to the examination specifications. 'Stand-alone' resources can also be used independently by students – for interest and enjoyment as much as for specific exam practice, which is a good thing to promote. Their disadvantage is that they are not always immediate – the news can be out of date, and sometimes very old indeed, although old copies can provide a useful bank of materials for students researching topics for their oral as well as their written coursework; in fact, listening to these resources is an extremely beneficial way for students both to understand the issues connected with their oral topics and to gather the types of phrase and vocabulary that they will want to use in their presentation.

Given the disadvantages of pre-selected texts, however, it is worth looking at other key sources for more current material, notably satellite or digital television, video recordings, radio, the Internet and the Foreign Language Assistant. These are explored below.

Using satellite or digital television and video

The advent of satellite television was a boon to language teaching classrooms and it is a major source of authentic listening material with many advantages:

- the images aid comprehension;
- there is an immediacy, particularly in regular news bulletins;
- there is a wide choice of programmes for all interests – news, day-time TV magazine programmes, documentaries, quiz show, series, etc.

To be used effectively, satellite or digital television should be:

- readily available to the students;
- linked up to a video recorder;
- advertised, with programme listings clear and highlighted;
- actively promoted by the teacher.

Probably the most useful type of satellite television material is the news report, either the regular nightly reports or the regular bulletins that occur throughout the day. They provide up-to-date insights into current affairs and events of particular interest to the target-language audience, and, as such, promote cultural awareness. Many of the advanced level topic areas are usually touched upon in each bulletin. Moreover, they are usually delivered in a standard, recognisable format with clear diction and employing the kind of formal language beloved of exam boards. If the news is recorded and available on video, practically all of the tasks suggested in the section earlier in this chapter on types of task (see p49) can be used – with pre-prepared materials and questions specific to the particular text if desired.

Using foreign language news: an example

If the news is live (or very recently recorded), then the lesson will follow a different – and often more dynamic – pattern than a lesson where everything is structured in advance, but the teacher can still have a number of tools at his or her disposal. A quick brainstorming on the board of what might appear in the news extract is a useful way to precede the actual viewing. To give students a focus for the viewing itself, the following standardised resource sheet can help prompt and structure note-taking (and provide material for a post-viewing discussion):

Using foreign language news

Nachrichten heute den ....

Bericht Titel?	Wer?	Wo?	Was?	Wie?	Warum?	Details?
1.						
2.						
3.						
4.						
5.						
6.						
7.						
8.						
9.						

Students should not feel discouraged if they have not completed every box – every news bulletin is different, and not every item lends itself to this sort of structuring. However, it does provide a framework which works more often than not. Once the news has been seen once (or more often, if recorded and if the teacher feels that this would be supportive to the students), the teacher can ask the students which items they found of most interest and these could become the focus of most of the rest of the lesson – students can share information about what they saw, ask questions about what they did not understand, check vocabulary and extend the discussion into opinions – for example, what did they think about the issues raised? Did they approve of the minister's decision? What other problems do they foresee if the unions are not given their way? After another failed marriage is explored at length, is now the time to abandon the cult of celebrity? All of this could be followed up by a post-viewing task designed to promote the strategies of synthesising and ordering information (see below).

(8)

(S)

resource sheet

Synthesizing and ordering information

Stellen Sie sich vor, Sie sind Redakteur einer Tageszeitung in Berlin.

Jeden Morgen müssen Sie entscheiden, welche Berichte in Ihrer Zeitung erscheinen sollten.

Wählen Sie drei Berichte aus den Satellitennachrichten, den Sie gerade zugehört haben, und schreiben Sie eine Rede, in der Sie Ihrem Redaktionsteam erklären:

• warum diese die Hauptgeschichten sind;

• welche Details die wichtigsten sind (und warum);

• wie die Geschichten in der Zeitung behandelt werden sollten.

For light relief, a similar sort of standardised format can be used to look at the adverts between programmes, again, whether live or recorded:

9
S

Werbung!

Schreiben Sie Ihre Antworte auf Deutsch.

Was wird beschrieben? (Name, Marke usw.)	Ist die Werbesendung schwer/einfach zu verstehen? Warum?	Was ist Ihre Meinung davon?
1.		
2.		
3.		
4.		
5.		
6.		
7.		

Noch ein paar Fragen:

- Haben diese Werbesendungen etwas miteinander gemeinsam?
- Sind diese Werbesendungen anders als britische Werbesendungen?
- Wie wichtig sind die Wörter darin?
- Wie wichtig sind die Bilder darin?
- Hat Sie noch etwas beeindruckt?

© CILT, the National Centre for Languages 2004

Other satellite programmes

News and adverts are not the only source of satellite material. Easy television listening and viewing can come from dubbed American TV series – of which there are many on satellite, particularly on the German channels – and this can be a good introduction to listening for pleasure. The context is familiar to students, the language is formulaic, the action is straightforward to understand and the dubbing makes for clear, usually accent-free target language.

They come with a caveat, however – they lack the stimulus of a cultural context set in the target country, and should be viewed with caution as a result. Balance of listening materials is essential!

Soap operas set in the target country, on the other hand, are a particularly rich source of listening material. They provide an insight into the culture and usually reflect everyday life.

Background details help develop students' awareness and understanding of the cultural context of the target-language country, and the language used is often recycled in various different ways as the same story is told and re-told to different characters by different people with a range of voices, accents and dialects.

Finally, quiz shows can be challenging to follow – because of the rules as much as the language and questions involved – but they are a good source of entertainment, and lighter tasks can include replaying them in class with the students as contestants. To be saved for a rainy day, perhaps!

The Internet as a source of listening material

The Internet offers a readily accessible way to listen to or watch real, everyday language in French, German and Spanish – as well as almost any other language you may like to hear. Since the software for on-line audio or video is free, it makes listening very easy – and usually much easier than conventional radio. Reception of conventional radio is, of course possible in some parts of the UK and it can also be recorded on a visit to the country. As a source of radio material, however, the Internet is hard to beat.

Virtually any computer made in the last few years, Mac or PC, is capable of using the software, and even an older computer with a relatively slow 100MHz processor, a sound card and a modem can play streaming audio from the Web (although a faster system is much better).

Minimum systems requirements (with ideal systems requirements in brackets) are usually:

- 400 MHz processor (**800 MHz or better**);
- 28.8 modem (**56K modem, ISDN, DSL, or cable modem**);
- soundcard;
- Windows 95 or 98/Mac OS8x (**Windows XP, MAC OS X**);
- 64MB of memory (**128MB or higher**);
- minimum 20MB of free hard disk space (**as much as possible**) ;
- free streaming software (RealPlayer, Media Player, QuickTime) (**'Plus' or 'Pro' versions with extra features**);
- a browser (Internet Explorer, Netscape, etc) configured with the proper plug-ins for various audio formats (.wav, .mp3, Real, etc).

Radio on the Internet

There are literally hundreds of stations available on-line – far too many to list here, although Appendix 4 contains a list of some of the websites where authentic foreign language radio broadcasts can be heard. All of these websites are directly accessible via the *Learning through listening* Web page: **www.cilt.org.uk/publications/learningthroughlistening**.

The advantage of accessing these texts is that there is an endless supply – variety is guaranteed. These sites also contain a mixture of recorded extracts, which can be listened to several times, and live broadcasts.

Students will find regular news bulletins (including recordings of the previous night's main stories), interviews, adverts, weather forecasts and songs). Texts vary in length but most fall within the 30 second to four to five minute band, which makes them ideal for advanced learners. Encourage your students to use them in one or more of the following ways:

- intensive listening, where students give their entire attention to the text (particularly suitable for recorded extracts which can be listened to several times) – they can practise individual listening strategies as they seek to understand all or most of the entire text;
- extensive listening for gist or familiarity with sounds;
- simply have the radio on in the background as the students use their computers for something else, as long as this does not interfere with their concentration;
- replace music with radio in a foreign language while the students play games or engage in mundane tasks around the house – this is an excellent way to

encourage listening and to help students absorb language and cultural soundbites such as advertising jingles.

Easy access to real time broadcasts means that there is no excuse for students not to listen!

Video on the Internet

Video on the Internet – on-line streaming – is less easily accessible than radio on the Internet: there are fewer sites (usually the main television channels – see Appendix 4), and depending on the speed of your computer processor and (crucially) your Internet connection, it can sometimes be frustrating. The definition of the images is usually less good than on video recordings from satellite.

Downloading clips which do not work can waste a lot of time if students are not careful, and should be used with caution. Set against this, however, is the ease of access – last night's news bulletin is only a few clicks of the mouse away and can be watched again and again without the need to rewind a video recorder. Programmes are often split into manageable chunks – the French channel TV5, for instance, offers the choice of watching the entire news bulletin or specific stories.

Perhaps the best way – for both teachers and students – is to experiment to find what works most effectively for each individual and how listening can be made as accessible as possible.

Other electronic media

Satellite, video and the Internet are the perhaps the easiest ways to access and collect authentic listening materials in a foreign language, but there are other electronic means, all of which have advantages and disadvantages, as shown in the table overleaf.

	Advantages	Disadvantages
Video/computer conferencing	■ conversation and discussion can take place with real native speakers ■ immediacy	■ can be complex and time-consuming to set up ■ requires state-of-the-art equipment ■ strong links needed with target-language schools, groups, etc
CD-ROMs	■ quicker to access than video ■ contain more non-verbal clues than cassette recordings	■ like pre-recorded cassettes and videos, materials are not necessarily up-to-date
Music – cassette, video, CD, Internet file	■ can give an insight into contemporary trends ■ can be listened to for pleasure	■ the poetic word can be obscure and the time needed to understand it can be out of proportion to its usefulness within a defined course ■ English is a dominant feature of music
Films	■ extend cultural awareness beyond everyday events ■ can be watched for pleasure	■ lengthy ■ often contain obscure or difficult to understand language

The disadvantages should not prevent you using these media, however, and you may find that your choice of one of the above allows you to tap effectively into the interests of your students. Films, for instance, can be used as the basis for a wider discussion. Use Resource sheet 10 opposite to draw together comprehension in questions 1–3, with the secondary tasks in questions 4–6 to broaden this understanding.

Native speakers and the Foreign Language Assistant

If students want to have constant, easy, varied, challenging and stimulating access to listening materials that demand their interaction, there is no real substitute for spending time in a foreign country. Given that it is usually impractical in the case of students studying for advanced level qualifications to spend extended periods of time abroad, making use of the authentic materials suggested above and contact with native speakers is the next best thing. When students do have the opportunity to talk with native speakers, however, they – and the native speaker – need to know how best to use the time to develop listening skills.

(10) (S) Crítica de una película

1. Anote el género, la fecha, el director, los actores principales y otros detalles que considere importantes.

2. Haga un resumen de la trama.

3. Escriba una crítica breve de la película (hasta un máximo de 100 palabras) teniendo en cuenta lo siguiente:
   - las actuaciones de los actores
   - el público a quién va dirigida
   - la música
   - los efectos especiales
   - la cinematografía
   - el ritmo de la acción
   - el guión

4. Haga una entrevista con un compañero de clase acerca de la película y grabe la conversación en casete o en video.

5. Escuche/mire su grabación, y analice su propia actuación. Discútalo con otros compañeros de clase y averigüe lo que piensan.

6. Escuche/mire las grabaciones de otros compañeros de clase. ¿Qué puede aprender de ellos? ¿Qué comentarios les haría?

The Foreign Language Assistant is often used as a substitute teacher, either because of over-direction from the teacher or through lack of direction, when the FLA is left to his or her own devices and needs to find something 'safe' – a text, usually, around which to base a lesson. A commonly observed pattern involves the FLA reading through a text with one or more students and picking out vocabulary. These lessons are intended to be the prelude to discussion along the lines of the discussion of an oral topic in the examination, but are often spent largely in silence, punctuated by questions posed by the FLA (and subsequently answered by him/her). It makes sense to use native speakers as a source of listening prompts to speaking and to exploit the potential he/she has to stimulate listening skills. The time with the FLA is a precious resource and is limited – it must not be wasted. The following guidelines may help your students to make best use of this resource.

resource sheet

Tips for Foreign Language Assistants: helping to develop listening

1. When planning tasks, remember that the focus of your lessons with these advanced level students is **listening** and **speaking**.

2. Avoid using lengthy written texts – in fact, a non-verbal or picture stimulus is much more appropriate.

3. Talk a lot! Less confident students will often not be ready to speak, so do not see this unwillingness to contribute as a failure – instead, they will use the opportunity with you to listen, so find ways of checking their comprehension non-verbally (*oui/non* answers, selecting information, pointing out information, etc). This is a particularly tricky area to judge – you must be sensitive to the needs and abilities of the individual students in front of you, to ensure that you are not preventing them from speaking when they are ready to. Get to know your students (discuss them with their teacher and observe them at work) and have reasonable expectations.

4. Be encouraging to students.

5. Consider using video clips, satellite news, etc. They provide a good visual focus and will stimulate discussion as well as being a listening resource. Discuss all of these resources with the main teacher of the class to make sure that they complement the ongoing programmes of strategy awareness and topic areas. Try to avoid turning them into reading exercises – make your instructions oral – and don't demand a written outcome.

© CILT, the National Centre for Languages 2004

12

S

resource sheet

How to get the most out of your Foreign Language Assistant (listening skills)

- Remember that your time with the FLA has two purposes – to improve **your speaking** and to improve **your listening**. Do not forget the latter!

- Listen carefully to everyone in the group, but especially to the FLA.

- Ask when you do not understand.

- If you have listened well, you will feel quite tired at the end of the session, even if you have not contributed much orally – use this as a guide to how much effort you need to put in!

© CILT, the National Centre for Languages 2004

When students go to the foreign country, on an exchange visit or for work experience, they can also be encouraged actively to develop their listening skills alongside their general language development and cultural awareness. The tips on Resource sheet 13 on p66 can be helpful for students.

Making the most of your time abroad: developing listening skills

- Go out of your way to listen to a range of different people talking about different things, for example:

    - pay attention to announcements – in supermarkets and railway stations;

    - listen to and participate in conversations with your host family as they talk about everything from everyday matters to political opinions;

    - eavesdrop on conversations in the bus, in the street and in cafes;

    - make a point of watching the evening news;

    - listen to the radio throughout the day if you can, and tune in to chat shows and quizzes on the television;

    - go to as many different events as you can – concerts, meetings, social occasions – so that you can listen to a wide range of voices in a variety of contexts.

- Note down words and phrases you hear and practise repeating them – this will increase your productive vocabulary as well as making it easier for you to learn to recognise the same or similar words in other aural contexts.

- Take the initiative – ask questions of people. If you ask more open-ended questions (*Pourquoi? Comment? Qu'est-ce que vous pensez de …?*) then you will stimulate lots of interesting opportunities for listening.

There is enormous scope for using 'home-grown' authentic listening materials on a regular basis in an advanced level course and in an inventive way. In the following case study Dave Padfield describes the advantages of this in practice and illustrates the ease with which teachers can create their own listening materials.

Case study

Creating and using authentic sources
Dave Padfield, Senior Lecturer in Languages, Plymouth Business School

- -

Several years ago, being generally disappointed with both the range and quality of listening materials which were commercially available for teachers of French, I decided to create my own. Initially, I recorded a great number of news items from

French radio stations and used these quite successfully. However, as they did not always correspond to the topics I wanted to target and, in addition, because I was anxious to bring authentic discussion of everyday topics in French into my classroom, I took the decision to adopt the guise of a 'roving reporter' and to compile my own bank of recordings. Equipped with cassette recorder and microphone, I devoted some of my holiday time in France to interviewing a certain number of friends and a selection of complete strangers, from a variety of backgrounds, on a wide range of topics. On my return home, I selected the best recordings, edited them as necessary and devised appropriate exercises for class use.

Creating and using materials in this way added another dimension to my teaching. An additional and totally unexpected bonus was that my students were very appreciative of the recordings because of their authenticity and vitality. I found the experience to be both immensely satisfying and rewarding and, being both the instigator of the conversations and the creator of the accompanying exercises, I could have a guiding hand in encouraging and supporting my students in:

- the comprehension of authentic language;
- the coverage of particular topics;
- their acquisition of vocabulary;
- their familiarisation with grammatical structures;
- the development of their fluency;
- the improvement of their accent;
- the raising of their level of confidence.

It goes without saying that there is an investment of time in the compilation of such materials. However, to my mind, the results justify the sacrifices which need to be made. This has been an on-going project of mine and over the last fifteen years I have progressively improved my interviewing technique and my recording equipment (now in digital format, on mini-disc). Such home-grown materials can be stimulating, informative and an excellent springboard to the learning process. In my experience, the use of recordings of 'real-life' conversations encourages the development of reflexes in the target language – students who have been introduced to language from authentic sources are thus less prone to native-language interference. This approach familiarises students with the natural pauses, the 'grunts and groans' of the language and allows them to learn new vocabulary in situ. They also hear grammar 'at work' in situations where it is used as a tool for effective communication. They can, as a result, analyse and better appreciate phrase and sentence structure at the same time as being encouraged to identify different accents and register.

Ways in which these recordings can be used are numerous – a brief look at recent examination papers at the appropriate level will reveal a wealth of different question styles. However, with a little thought, it is possible to devise one's own particular ways and means of assessing comprehension of the stimulus material and the ability to present or manipulate it. I use the materials I gather with the following exercise formats:

- written questions (in English or in the target language, requiring answers in the same language) to establish comprehension;
- as material for a résumé of the conversation (again, in English or in the target language);
- gap-fill exercises using the full transcript with certain key words missing (I would suggest about twenty gaps). This is a good exercise to test grammar – correct use of verbs, adjectives, etc);
- multiple-choice questions;
- 'finding the partner' – beginnings and endings of sentences which need to be matched up (again, a good way of testing comprehension and grammatical control);
- 'true/false' – questions need to be carefully selected and phrased in order to avoid the task being too easy;
- 'complete the sentence ...!' – the giving of half a sentence (either beginning or ending) to which the student adds information as considered necessary;
- 'find the adjectives/adverbs/passive constructions ...!' – a useful grammatical tool;
- finding synonyms/antonyms – words/definitions are given, students have to find their equivalents used in the interview;
- open oral discussion of the content of the recording ... eliciting factual information and/or opinions from those who have listened to a particular interview;
- written exercises based on the content of the interview;
- starting points for research (maybe using Internet sources) into the things mentioned during the interview.

It must not be forgotten that transcripts can, additionally, be used for individual or in-class study (with or without the recording). A real advantage is that the cassettes/CDs and worksheets are not subject to a publisher's copyright (the creator being the copyright holder; however, consent must of course be obtained from the speakers when making the recordings). This means that the materials can be extensively copied and subsequently used for self-study wherever the user happens to wander with his or her personal stereo!

I think that the many students who have used my 'home-grown' materials have become more inquisitive, perceptive and creative in their use of language and this has been a key factor in their motivation and their success.

Progression in listening and how to achieve it

It is tempting to think that a programme to improve listening skills can start with less complex texts and tasks and proceed to more complex ones, but in practice this does not work: students will encounter all sorts of different aural stimuli throughout the time they are studying for an advanced level course, and it would be counter-productive to limit this exposure as part of a master plan to provide linear progression. Moreover, as is clear above, the science of deciding whether texts and tasks are easy or complex is a very inexact one, and depends as much on the learners as it does on the intrinsic nature of the material.

Practice and wide exposure, then, provided that all the text and task types are covered adequately, are probably the best way to ensure progression, and because so much will depend on the students themselves listening beyond the bounds of the classroom, perhaps the most important step that advanced learners can take to improve their listening skills is to learn to relax and enjoy listening in a foreign language. If they do, they will reduce the anxiety that can hinder examination performance in particular, and they will more naturally listen to the range of texts that they need in order to have the right level of exposure. While this is easier said than done, there are various things that teachers can do to help students on the way.

Creative ways of integrating listening into daily life – learning to love listening!

For students to integrate listening into a daily routine, they are likely to need some prompting from the teacher, unless they are very well-motivated indeed – and even so, they will need encouragement. The following ideas on Resource sheet 14 (p70) can be fed into students when it seems appropriate for them to adopt them.

14

Useful tips to improve your listening daily

- Check out **www.cilt.org.uk/publications/learningthroughlistening** for a set of links to Internet radio websites.

- Save as one of your 'Favourites' on the computer your preferred Internet foreign radio website and a site that lists which programmes are on and when. Have the radio on in the background as you work or do other things, and make a point of spending some time listening intensively and with specific goals.

- Decide with other students in your group what time you will all watch the news together.

- Save as one of your 'Favourites' on the computer your preferred foreign TV station and make a regular time to listen to the previous night's news – first thing in the morning might work.

- When learning vocabulary, make it a habit to record new words on to tape. Play them back regularly to help you remember them aurally, and to help develop your auditory perception.

- When reading a written text, read parts of it aloud.

Creating individual listening programmes

If it is to be successful, the programme to improve listening skills followed by each student will be different. They may share the same premises – the central listening strategies, the target language itself – and they may use the same tools to prompt initial discussion and to evaluate progress, but they will vary vastly depending on the needs of the students. It is the role of the teacher to ensure, through regular monitoring of texts and tasks other than those covered in class, that the interests of each student, while encouraged, do not prevent him or her from being exposed to the whole range of material appropriate at advanced level study. Regular checking using Resource sheet 5 – Tracking progress (p41) will go some way to seeing that this happens.

Evaluating skills and tracking progress

Regular evaluation – perhaps at the end of every topic area – is essential if students are to become more aware of their explicit strategy usage. They need to be able to understand what they are doing, how well they are doing it, and whether they are improving. This will be motivating and will also allow them to plan their continued development. Teachers can also use the information gained from an evaluation process to help them gauge what has been successful in the programme and what has worked less well, which will help them to select appropriate texts for future classes.

Resource sheet 2 in Appendix 1 (pp91–94) can be adapted to form the basis of an evaluation task and subsequent discussion. This resource sheet – Assessing strategic competence in listening – is also a good way to check how much progress students feel they have made in understanding what is required of them to be better listeners. Equally, Resource sheet 4 – Evaluating listening skills (p40) – contains an alternative set of questions which can be adapted for evaluation purposes. It is important that students have the opportunity to explore for themselves what they are doing and how their listening is improving, but it is equally important for them to have the chance to discuss this with the teacher, and for the teacher to give guidance and advice. Classes of advanced level language learners contain a wide range of students with differing degrees of self-awareness and teachers need to tailor their advice to the individual. In evaluating progress, teachers should ask the following questions:

- Has the student listened to a sufficiently wide range of texts, both those set by the teacher and those he/she has listened to independently? (Evidence from Resource sheet 5 – Tracking progress on p41.)
- Does the student show signs of increased strategy awareness in discussing listening? (Evidence from teacher observation and conversations with the student.)
- Are the student's independent listening habits developing? (Evidence from conversations with the student.)
- Have you noticed an improvement in his or her listening in class?
- Can you identify which strategies a particular student would benefit from adopting?

Integrating listening into a wider scheme of work

Inevitably, the focus of much of this book has been on the development of a listening skills programme, but practicalities – time and the other demands of the advanced level course – mean that this cannot exist in isolation from other aspects of language learning. In fact, it would be counter-productive for it to do so: a programme to develop listening skills will also develop other learning skills and increase general language learning strategy awareness. If it is integrated well into a scheme of work, it will complement reading skills and prompt the development of writing and speaking skills.

Armed with all the advice and ideas in this and previous chapters about possible approaches to a listening strategies programme, appropriate types of text and task and sources of material, the teacher or Head of department needs to consider:

- the balance of time available for listening in a scheme of work;
- the learners and their needs;
- access to sources;
- time available for preparation;
- division of labour within the department.

For a Head of department looking to revamp completely the scheme of work used post-16, the following flowchart may help focus the mind:

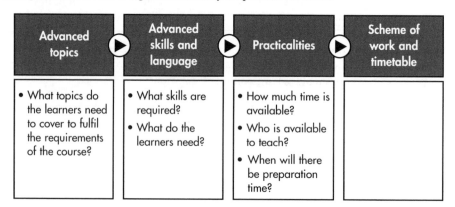

The topics will depend on the exam board, and guidelines for advanced skills and language can be found in the breakdown of the assessment objectives in the exam-board specifications. However, the following five-point scheme may be helpful in allocating time to areas of study throughout the two years of an advanced level course. The five sections – Listening and reading, Speaking and writing, Cultural awareness, Awareness of skills and strategies and Exam skills – are in roughly equal proportion, although it is clear that the later sections, particularly the awareness of skills and strategies, feed into and can be incorporated into the earlier sections of the main language skills.

Listening and reading
- range of skills from gist to precise listening;
- understanding authentic texts;
- developing opinions in response to texts.

Speaking and writing
- accuracy of productive language;
- fluency of language;
- expressing ideas in a structured fashion.

Cultural awareness
- knowing about the country;
- knowing what is going on.

Awareness of skills and strategies
- grammar skills;
- reading and listening;
- independent learning.

Exam skills
- coping with timings and lengths of exercise;
- practising exercise types (summary etc).

A good scheme of work will vary from year to year and will adapt according to the needs and abilities of the individual learners in that particular year. In practice, in order to manage the course and devote time throughout the year to learners rather than to materials development, teachers need to have some kind of structure and a bank of resources and strategies that can be flexible but nonetheless give some stability. Listening strategy development will vary from year to year depending on the learners, but the structure can be built into a scheme of work as a strand running throughout the year or two years of an advanced level course. Teachers will have a successful listening skills programme at their disposal if they:

- possess a set of tools to stimulate discussion and awareness of strategies;
- give the students access to information about strategies;
- provide students with a variety of listening resources (and encourage them to find their own);
- and build in regular evaluation and advice.

Good luck!

key points

- A wide range of listening texts and tasks is available to the teacher and student at advanced level; texts and tasks currently in use as part of a scheme of work can be audited according to rough levels of difficulty in order to identify gaps in the material presented to students.

- Authentic texts are readily accessible via satellite television, the Internet, native speakers and other sources (including 'ready-made' cassette and video resources, films, etc) and their use should be encouraged.

- Materials preparation can be kept to a minimum by using resource sheets which have a standard, multi-purpose format that students can use to assemble information and thoughts on their listening strategies for further discussion.

- Progression needs to be carefully monitored and evaluated by students and teachers.

- Time taken to integrate listening into a scheme of work is time well spent!

Listening in the exam: Hints, tips and guidance

The previous three chapters have been devoted to the general skill of listening at advanced level, to the strategies learners need to develop in order to improve and to meet the requirements of the A level, and to the exploitation of appropriate texts in a way that encourages our students to become better listeners. Listening tasks should not, as a matter of course, be listening tests – learners need to have the space and time to practise the discrete strategies that will help them develop. As the examinations approach, however, it is important that students gain enough practice in the type of task likely to be set by the exam boards. Students will also need to adopt particular approaches to help them prepare for the rigours of the tests they will face (see also Advanced Pathfinder 3: *Tests and targets* (Neather 2001) for additional suggestions).

Preparing for the examination – shifting from learning to examination practice

If listening strategy development is to be effective, it should not focus at too early a stage on examination preparation. Examination texts and questions demand a complex range of strategies, and have the added pressure of anxiety, which can interfere with students' abilities to listen successfully and to improve their listening by self-evaluation. However, a good listening strategies programme will include not only a wide range of the types of text and task illustrated in Chapter 3, but also, as the examination approaches, opportunities for students to become fully aware of the likely format that they will encounter in the exam room, and opportunities to practise and test themselves.

A level examination listening texts – what will the exam boards produce?

The texts that students will encounter in their final examinations will have as their focus the topics specified by the exam boards, and it is essential that students are aware of these, although in practice they will find that they draw on general topic areas as much as specific ones for their understanding. Types of text again are specified by the exam boards and will include the following:

- news items,
- telephone messages,
- announcements,
- advertisements,
- interviews,

- radio talks,
- reviews,
- conversation,
- discussions,
- current affairs broadcasts.

The texts will vary in length from around fifteen seconds to one to two minutes, and on average, students should expect to listen to around five minutes' worth of material for a 90 minute exam; again, however, teachers should always check the latest examination specifications carefully and make sure that their students are fully aware of what they are likely to find.

A course handbook can be a useful way of communicating this and the other essentials that students need to know but which teachers do not want to dwell on at length throughout the course itself, and is a document that students can keep throughout the duration of the course. A good handbook might contain an overview of the aims of the Advanced level course, an outline of the modules to be covered, a brief scheme of work and details of the sort of assessment techniques that students will face. There is scope, too, for anything else the teacher feels appropriate – a glossary, perhaps, of exam phrases, and details of the types of task that students may face in the examination.

A level examination tasks – what could the exam boards demand?

A level boards have at their disposal a wide range of question types, requiring:

- true/false/not in text responses,
- non-verbal responses,
- one word answers,
- multiple choice,
- selection of words from a bank of words to fill a gap,
- full sentence responses.

Interpreting may be an examination option open to students, and this is a specialised skill which requires particular practice. It is also an excellent way of focusing listening and training the ear; see Appendix 2 (p95) for a case study where interpreting is used in the classroom.

Students should not overlook listening in preparing for their oral exams: the task of listening is almost as important as the task of producing language in the oral exam, and preparation for listening and oral exams can often be done alongside one another, as Anneli McLachlan (2001) demonstrates in Advanced Pathfinder 1: *Advancing oral skills*. Students should be prepared for the type of listening task that they might encounter in their oral exam:

- response to questions on a prepared topic;
- response to questions on an unprepared topic;
- discussion led by the student (presentation);
- conversation;
- role-play;
- interpreting.

The level of difficulty of the listening task at AS and A level is affected more by the difficulty of the text or what the examiner says than by the student's ability to produce correct language at an appropriate level. Inevitably, however, a number of listening tasks demand answers in the target language (most especially in the oral!), and in such cases the ability to communicate comprehension is as important as the comprehension itself. In preparation for these questions, students need to link their listening proficiency to their proficiency in writing if they are to gain the highest marks. They will be most successful, however, if their primary focus is to use their listening strategies to understand the text first rather than being distracted by the questions, although questions can provide useful guidance to aid comprehension, and ultimately need to be answered correctly! We go on below to suggest useful approaches to the tasks.

Tackling different types of task – hints and procedures

When students are practising examination tasks, they may find the following guidelines helpful. These link the strategies identified earlier (in Chapter 2) for learning listening through targeted practice with the demands of the exam; students who have become familiar with the strategies and can see how useful they are will be able to apply them effectively in response to examination questions. The aim, of course, is to listen and understand as swiftly and efficiently as possible, and this is where the use of strategies is helpful. Certain strategies work best on certain types of task, and some guidance as to which students may find helpful in an exam is given in Checklist 8 on p78.

Task	Before beginning the paper.

Strategy	• ADVANCE ORGANISATION

(see p26)

If students read the paper thoroughly, they will gain an overview of the tasks required and this will help them to anticipate the language they are likely to hear. An awareness of the topic areas and the issues to be discussed helps to prompt vocabulary recall..

Task	True/false/not in text responses. Non-verbal responses. One word answers. Multiple choice. Selection of words from a bank of words to fill a gap.

Strategy	• SELECTIVE ATTENTION

(see p26)

For these types of question, students need to decide in advance to pay attention to specific aspects of language input or situation, listening for 'cues' that will help them find the right answer. For example, in a question that asked for true or false answers, the student would listen out for the main word or words in the statement provided in the question, and be prepared to hear a synonym or a rephrasing of the statement. Once the student has found the part of the listening text where these words occur, he or she can listen more closely to determine the stance the speaker is taking and then make a decision about whether the statement is true or false. In a word-fill exercise, the student will find it easiest to answer the questions if he or she makes a point of reading carefully all the words from the bank given and the paragraph into which they are to be inserted, and using this to help prompt ideas of the sorts of words that might come up in the text. This prepares the ground for listening and makes it much more likely that the student will understand the text.

checklist

© CILT, the National Centre for Languages 2004

8

Strategies for listening in different types of exam task (contd)

Task	**Full sentence responses.** **Exercises that demand a productive response to the whole listening text.**
Strategy	For these questions, there are a number of strategies which students might find helpful:
(see p26)	• DIRECTED ATTENTION, i.e. deciding in advance to focus on the specific task and to avoid irrelevant distractors, listening out for the 'gist' of the text and the main ideas.
(see p28)	• DELAYED PRODUCTION, i.e. consciously deciding to postpone responding to a text to concentrate on understanding the whole text. This can be a useful way into a text, and is usually more effective when combined with a pre-reading of the questions, which again will help to situate the text in context and will prompt vocabulary recall.
(see p31)	• NOTE-TAKING, i.e. writing down the main idea, important points, outline or summary of information presented orally – this can take a little longer, and may mean that some irrelevant information is recorded, but it can help some students gain a very good idea of what is happening in the text, and if this gives them the confidence to be able to answer the questions more quickly, it is an appropriate strategy.

Task	**Coping with unknown language in the paper.**
Strategy	This aspect of the listening paper calls into action a range of strategies which are just as useful in responding to other elements of the exam papers:
(see p30)	• TRANSLATION, i.e. using the first language as a base for understanding the second language.
(see p31)	• DEDUCTION, i.e. consciously applying rules to understand the second language.

Task	Coping with unknown language in the paper. (Continued)
Strategy (see p33)	• CONTEXTUALISATION, i.e. locating a word or phrase in a meaningful language sequence.
(see p34)	• ELABORATION, i.e. relating new information to other concepts already memorised.
(see p34)	• TRANSFER, i.e. using previously acquired linguistic and/or conceptual knowledge to help make listening easier.
(see p34)	• INFERENCING, i.e. using available information to guess meanings of new items, predict outcomes, or fill in missing information.

Task	Checking after answering the questions in the paper.
Strategy	Checking is essential to pick up any gaps missed or any misunderstandings, and the following strategies are useful in identifying any areas that still need work:
(see p28)	• SELF-MONITORING, i.e. looking critically at any assumptions made and checking carefully and methodically for accuracy and appropriateness.
(see p28)	• SELF-EVALUATION, i.e. seeing if you feel happy with the outcome – are there any sections where the meaning is still a little unclear or the answers don't quite seem to make sense? If so, these sections need to be re-visited if there is time.

checklist

The best preparation for exam success is long term. In the following case study, Tatiana Dayre, Head of Russian at one of Northern Ireland's largest grammar schools, describes how she encourages the development of listening strategies and proficiency in her AS Russian students. She is explicit in her use of a number of the strategies identified in Chapter 2 and clearly uses them with great success to focus on the demands of the listening elements of the exam.

Case study

Preparing for the exam
Tatiana Dayre, Head of Russian, Methodist College, Belfast

Students' different ability levels

At the College there are normally about five to ten students in Russian AS and A2 classes. Students starting the AS course are not native speakers but have followed and passed a four-year GCSE course (a minimum of two hours of Russian per week). The AS group is normally a mixed ability one: there are 'non-coursework' students who have achieved A* in all four skills at GCSE examinations and also students with B grades whose written paper at GCSE was coursework. It is important to point out that students face different demands at GCSE, depending on whether they opt for written coursework or the Writing Paper in the examination. In the course of their final GCSE year, students opting for coursework are required to produce three pieces of written work, only one of which must be done under examination conditions. For the other two, students can work at home using a dictionary, coursebooks and other aids. Students who opt for the Writing paper in the exam are required to produce two pieces in one hour without using dictionaries or other additional material. This means that the range of vocabulary and complexity of grammar skills can vary considerably between the two groups of students. This has significant repercussions for the training and development of listening skills at AS level.

Listening skills at GCSE and at AS

The GCSE specification certainly places emphasis on listening to ascertain both gist and detail of the language, yet the multiple choice format of responding does not, in my opinion, ensure the comprehensive communication required by students as they seek to acquire the higher qualification. Students answering Section A at GCSE level (questions and answers in Russian) can achieve commendable results without understanding what the conversations are about. They can recognise the spoken word and successfully match it to a word on the answer sheet or simply tick the boxes randomly and still achieve 2 or 3 points out of a possible 6. In neither case has an adequate level of comprehension been achieved. Section B (questions and answers in English) tends to be more challenging because students have to listen for the whole message and understand most of it to be able to translate and answer the question. It is this skill of understanding the message that I try to develop with my AS students. The principle, therefore is that listening skills should be trained on the basis of vocabulary acquisition and handling of grammar.

Building up vocabulary

The initial task of the AS teacher is to rid the student of the dangerous reflex of ticking a box on the basis of a vaguely heard word. The second, which follows naturally, is training in the art of listening for content and here the key is vocabulary. One cannot hope to develop understanding without a strong grounding in vocabulary. With AS students I start with the *Tranzit* coursebook and the modest ambition of incrementally expanding and consolidating the students' vocabulary base. The first topic is celebrations/events in Russia and my aim here is to revise familiar GCSE words: Christmas, January, presents, parents, children, snow and cold and introduce new verbs: 'to put' (verb of motion) 'to decorate', 'to celebrate' and then introduce Russian reflexive verbs expressing emotions (to enjoy, to laugh, etc). On average pupils are able to recognise twenty new words in 60 minutes of intense teaching and learning. With three 60-minute lessons a week it should be possible for students to have 30 new words which they are able to incorporate into everyday usage and another 30 with which they will be familiar.

Contextualisation and grammar

Learning is aided by contextualisation. I make up a story about Russian Christmas and by using visual cues students can more quickly understand the message (e.g. draw Father Christmas and a Christmas tree on the board, decorate it and place presents under it). They are able to translate accurately what I say although they find it difficult to remember the actual words for decorating, laughing, or celebrating and the visual cues clearly enhance recall of the words. Recognition is also promoted by asking a student to mime the new words, including verbs. Teaching grammar alongside new vocabulary gives me the possibility of changing activity from listening to vocabulary to listening to verb or case endings. In the same lesson, we revise the verbs of motion with the accusative case, taking 'to put' as an example, and the conjugation of Russian reflexive verbs, e.g. 'to laugh'. In the case of presents lying under the tree, students observe the absence of a verb of motion and hence observe the use of the instrumental case after the preposition 'under'. The switch to grammar gives them a little rest from intense listening and gives me the opportunity to repeat verbs through questioning. Some students find the combination of grammar and vocabulary difficult to retain but at the end of the lesson they are encouraged to summarise what they learnt best and what they need to focus on in homework.

This system allows less able students to extend their vocabulary, while the others can revise grammar along with the new words and do not feel bored with monotonous drilling. Able linguists remember not only single words but also phrases, even sentences. They memorise prepositions and case endings and are therefore able to make up a fairly respectable 'Christmas paragraph' of their own by the end of the lesson.

I always use the more able students as a walking tape. They are placed in the 'hot seat' and students can check their knowledge by asking about vocabulary and grammar learnt during the lesson. An alternative is playing the 'Weakest link', where one student devises the questions based on vocabulary or grammar. The person who plays the questioner has to prepare a bank of questions (the number of questions depends on the person's ability, the nature of the coursebook chapter and the quantity of material learnt.) Questions may be based on any aspect of language learnt in the chapter. In our example of celebrations/events in Russia, the questioner may ask in Russian for some contextual knowledge, e.g. dates of a particular anniversary in the country or when the battle of Borodino occurred.

Alternatively, some questions may be based on grammar: for example, what case follows a certain verb studied in the chapter, or what preposition is used with a particular verb. In addition some questions may be based on Russian *faux amis* (words sounding similar in Russian but having different meanings). For example, the Russian adjective 'lyooboy' has nothing to do with the word 'lyoobov' (love) but simply means 'any'; 'droogoy', is not connected with 'droog' (friend) but is an adjective meaning 'different, another'. This type of *faux ami* is often used by the examiners who set Russian AS listening and reading papers. If the participant answers a question wrongly, the questioner gives the answer, but the question can be used again later in the game, thus encouraging students to listen and remember.

The game works well in a small class, especially as an end-of-unit revision test. It is surprising how much information, and what degree of detail, is remembered by the questioning student. However, I find this type of peer activity rewarding for both parties.

One further point about the game is that it provides an interesting and useful added value for the AS student – they can develop the skill of coping with an academic task under the spotlight of pressure.

Homework

The type of homework typically linked to these lessons would entail students writing up, in Russian, a story on the current topic and then presenting it in class for everyone else to translate. I normally ask students who read their stories, to produce a task for their listeners, for example, to answer, in English, five questions based on the story. The questions should prompt as much detail in the answers as possible and at least one should start with 'why'.

Returning to the topic of celebrations/events in Russia, students may ask a question such as: why was the child unhappy and why did it start to cry, or why did Masha receive more presents than Sasha, who was nevertheless laughing? I find answering 'why' questions important for developing understanding of the context. They can also set summary tasks. If a student's story consists of 150 words they can ask their listeners to produce a summary of no more than 60 words, but including the main points which they write on the board. Sometimes students just set open-ended tasks, such as 'translate what you hear'.

In this instance, students normally read their stories twice and they can repeat certain sentences if asked to. The competition engendered by a task emanating from a fellow student encourages them to incorporate as much of the new vocabulary and grammar as possible into their stories. This gives me the opportunity to correct the grammar of the student who set the task, while the others use it as a listening and translation activity set by the speaker. Afterwards they mark each other's work and I can use the time to work individually with students on the generalisation of the grammar rule studied.

As soon as the students realise that skills are transferable they become more productive when learning independently, e.g. they can put an unfamiliar word into the initial nominative case, find it in the dictionary, and deduce the word's gender, or its conjugation.

Developing examination skills

I find that these listening/translating activities develop students' examination skills and techniques. They have a much better idea of what to expect in the last task of AS Listening Paper. If, for example their summaries are longer than 60 words, the peer examiner draws a line at this point and stops marking. They often argue that they put the most important information at the end of their summary and feel penalised when this is not taken into account by the examiner. Through this process they learn quickly what points are most important in the summary and how to express them succinctly. Their disappointment not only acts as a good reminder about the organisation of the summary but also later on, focuses their letter writing skills in AS Unit 2.

These activities also help them in the grammar exercise of the listening exam paper. At AS level this is normally worth 6 points and is devised in such a way that students who have little idea of grammar will lose valuable marks no matter how attentively they listen to the tape. Students with a good understanding of grammar have a natural advantage on this task. If, for example, there is a blank space after a verb of motion, only a noun with the accusative ending can follow it and there is normally only one such possibility among the given words. Thus identifying parts of speech and learning grammatical rules are as important as the knowledge and recognition of vocabulary for maximising success in the Russian listening paper.

When practising listening skills I regard the use of tapes as the final task rather than the initial one. One must guard against students opting for the easy solution by using given transcripts of tapes, e.g. in the *Tranzit* pack, to answer questions on listening tasks. To this end I always add to the listening task and insist on the complete translation of the text. They always know that understanding of each word within the whole text will be required and checked.

The *Tranzit* coursebook, which I use as the main resource for AS students, contains the transcripts of all listening exercises. At the beginning of the year each student receives a coursebook and a tape from the Russian department. However, when the students are doing past listening papers as mock examinations they do not have transcripts. Sometimes they can have access to these when we are checking their results in class or when they are marking their peers.

When it comes to preparation for the listening examination paper a review of past papers is useful. Russian examiners, like all others, have their favourite words and structures. The examination board with which I'm most familiar regularly features verbs such as 'to develop, 'to increase, and 'to decrease'. They can be in their transitive (to develop something), intransitive or reflexive forms (economy develops itself). Particular themes are consistently present, e.g. the world of work, with the predictable vocabulary of salary, unemployment, workers, trade, product, to sell, to buy and all their synonyms. Therefore preparation by the teacher, through a careful analysis of past papers, is every bit as important as the effort expended by the students.

A guiding principle for the teacher is to develop in students what is known in the world of counselling as active listening. Students should be encouraged to attend to every aspect of the spoken word, including the tone of voice, inflection and rhythm. Through imaginative exercises and activities, they attend to vocabulary, grammatical structures and contextual meaning. If this can be achieved, then in the listening examination the impact of a lack of understanding in one area, e.g. an unfamiliar word, can be minimised through a broad knowledge of structures and rules. Hopefully this leads to the desired outcome sought by teacher, pupil and parents alike of maximising the final grade.

A2 students of Russian in Methodist College have only five 30-minute lessons compared to the seven lessons at AS. Therefore most of their listening has to be done independently at home. At the beginning of the term they are given listening packs with past examination listening papers. Most of these papers are old A level ones and date back as far as 1990. Students are expected to complete four listening examination papers per term. They are also given a listening tape from *Kompass* – the coursebook I use at A2 level.

Kompass, to my mind, provides a good continuation from *Tranzit* and all the listening scripts are included in the book. Often listening homework is set from the coursebook whereas the past listening papers are used for assessment and mock examinations. The extensive groundwork carried out at AS level comes into its own at this stage, because unlike the situation that existed until 2001, students are no longer permitted a dictionary in the examination room. By the end of the A2 course students of Russian need to learn sufficient vocabulary to be able to recognise it and use it to complete their examination papers without the help of the dictionary. This thorough learning of vocabulary and the basic rudiments of grammar, I believe, provide a firm foundation for their further studies at University level and for becoming professional linguists.

As the exam approaches: learning and preparation strategies

As this case study shows, preparing for the listening and oral examination consists of much more than just revising vocabulary and grammar – it is the skills themselves which must be practised. Checklist 9 opposite contains a few hints for students to help them focus effectively on the examinations ahead of them.

Tips for preparing for the exam

- Don't leave learning until the last minute!
- Keep listening to new texts and practising new language aloud – you will continue to make links and associations in your mind, and will be reinforcing previously learned language as you do so.
- Practise exam-type questions and time yourself. Don't let this become your sole means of practising listening, as you will not learn as much about listening if you only ever do timed exercises – keep practising a range of strategies. You do, however, also need to practise the techniques you will need to listen effectively in the exam, timing yourself, practising with the sorts of exercises you will encounter, etc.

Advice for students: the days and nights before

- Relax. If you are relaxed, you will find it much easier to remember associated words and ideas, and this will help you much more quickly gain an overall understanding of the passages.
- Enjoy listening to the foreign language. This will help you both relax and become more confident in your listening skills. You will keep learning right up until the last minute – this is good!
- Go into the exam with your head full of French/German/Spanish, having listened to or watched the news in the foreign language the previous evening and that morning, and having avoided English (including music) as much as possible.

In the exam ...

- Read all the questions carefully and underline the key words. See what clues you can pick up about what you are about to hear. Try to anticipate some of the vocabulary that might crop up in the text.
- Pay particular attention to what is required of you in the questions – are you asked to provide one or two examples? In multiple-choice questions, are you being asked to pick the item that is true or the one that is not?
- Answer as fully as possible but keep your answers clear and legible. Full sentences are generally not needed, but give as much detail as you can. If asked to mention two items and you can think of three, write down all three. When asked to give times or measurements, don't forget to specifiy the time of day or the unit of measurement.
- Look carefully at the number of marks and make sure you make the corresponding number of points.

checklist

© CILT, the National Centre for Languages 2004

Using a personal stereo or mini-CD player

As with any form of technology, practice makes perfect, and in the weeks (and preferably months) before the exam, students need to ensure that they have easy access to the machine they will actually use. This way they can become used to its idiosyncrasies and can feel confident that they can exploit its full potential to make their life easier in the exam. The tips on Checklist 10 may help a student to make most effective use of their player.

Tips on using a personal stereo or mini-CD player

- Have a piece of scrap paper to hand.
- ALWAYS zero the counter at the beginning of the tape if you have a mechanical player.
- When you start listening to each extract or text, write down the number of the text and where it appears on the counter. For digital players, remember that the introduction may count as Item 1, so to avoid being caught out, get into the habit well before the exam of automatically recording number of text and place on the tape/CD.
- Always look closely at the counter when you are rewinding – if you are distracted, you will end up rewinding and fast-forwarding much more than is necessary, and this will waste time.
- PLAN YOUR TIME CAREFULLY – look at the beginning of the exam to see how many texts there are and (if you are given this information) how long each one is. Dividing up your time is a balance between allocating time based on the length of the texts and allocating time based on the marks available for the question. There is no need for a complex calculation – just be constantly aware of how much you have left to do, and keep a careful eye on the time. If you always build in some checking time, you will be able to come back to your earlier questions, and it is far better to do this than not to attempt later questions. Listen to the texts in the order they come in the paper to save rewinding and fast-forwarding time – and work quickly!
- To help you answer efficiently, you may find it useful to follow this procedure for each text:
  1. take notes if you want during the first listening – do not write your answers yet;
  2. write most of your answers during the second listening;
  3. if you are stuck on one question, keep going – do not waste time;
  4. move on to the next text – you can return to this text at the end, and use further playings of the text to check your answers.

Developing listening beyond advanced level

All teachers like to feel that if they have been successful with their students, they will continue to develop and enjoy the language beyond the bounds of the classroom and the course, and will continue to listen either for fun, for intellectual stimulation or because the skill of understanding a spoken foreign language proves useful for a career or further education. We cannot insist on any of these, but here are some useful pointers for students that might help to encourage them along this path:

checklist

Preparing for language learning beyond school: developing your listening

If you are intending to study languages at university, then listening is a key skill that you will need, and it will largely be assumed that your listening skills are already well advanced before you get there. Prepare yourself before you embark on your course, and you will be relaxed, focused and ahead of the game!

What can you do to prepare?

- Keep listening to the radio – every day, more than once a day. Have the radio on in the background as you do other things and make time to listen to your favourite programmes (if you listen often enough, you will soon find you have one!).

- Make a date with the news on satellite – every evening!

- Take a sneak preview at the course content for your university course and listen out for related items on the radio or television.

- Talk to yourself – you will practise the phrases you hear other people saying and this will improve both your speaking and your ability to understand others.

- Enjoy it!

Languages in the world of work – how to keep ahead of the game by listening

Why?

Language proficiency is an invaluable career skill, and if you can understand what other people are saying in a foreign language, you will be putting yourself in an advantageous position when it comes to that promotion or pay rise. Not to mention the fact that interpreting can be very well paid!

Preparing for language learning beyond school: developing your listening (contd)

checklist

How?

- Target your listening to topics related to the area of work you are interested in or involved in, for example:
  - business news updates,
  - relevant documentaries,
  - trade materials,
  - relevant adverts.
- Listen to or watch the news every day – you need to know what is going on in the country.
- Organise relevant work experience and use the opportunity to pick up everything you need to know:
  - eavesdrop on employees talking about work and on the phone,
  - sit in on interviews,
  - engage in conversation: ask lots of questions and listen to the responses.

© CILT, the National Centre for Languages 2004

key points

- If listening strategy development is to be effective, it should not focus at too early a stage on exam preparation.
- Knowledge and familiarity with the paper and types of examination text and task are essential.
- Some of the strategies identified in Chapter 2 for improving listening can be adapted for use in an examination.
- Mental preparation the night before an exam – relaxing and enjoying listening to the news in the foreign language – makes a difference!
- Teachers can help their students develop a love of listening that will take them beyond advanced level.

Appendix 1:
Developing strategic competence in listening – further resource materials

Assessing strategic competence in listening

The purpose of this questionnaire is to help you think about what you do when you listen and when you try to improve your listening. People listen in different ways, and you may find it useful to identify what works best for you and to consider different ways of listening.

1. Think carefully about all your experiences of listening in a foreign language. Think about how you listen and how you seek to improve your listening. What do you do to help you listen, and what do you find useful? Tick one circle on each line below:

	always	often	sometimes	rarely	never
I decide in advance what I am going to listen to and how I am going to listen to it.	◯	◯	◯	◯	◯
I concentrate only on listening while I am doing it, and I do not get distracted.	◯	◯	◯	◯	◯

© CILT, the National Centre for Languages 2004

Assessing strategic competence in listening (contd)

	always	often	sometimes	rarely	never
I concentrate on listening only to the important parts of the text.	○	○	○	○	○
I know how I listen best, and I make sure that I listen in this way.	○	○	○	○	○
Before I listen to new words, phrases, and themes or concepts, I remind myself of similar words, phrases, themes or concepts that I already know.	○	○	○	○	○
I correct myself when I speak or write the new language I have heard.	○	○	○	○	○
I check later that I have learned the new language properly.	○	○	○	○	○
I repeat the new language aloud or in my head.	○	○	○	○	○
I try to explain it in French/German/Spanish to help me remember.	○	○	○	○	○
I imagine hearing again the new language I have encountered.	○	○	○	○	○
I translate into my first language.	○	○	○	○	○

resource sheet

2

S

Assessing strategic competence in listening (contd)

	always	often	sometimes	rarely	never
I try to remember new language in a group with other similar words or ideas.	○	○	○	○	○
I write new language down and make notes.	○	○	○	○	○
I use my knowledge of French/German/Spanish to help me understand the new words or grammar.	○	○	○	○	○
I make up a sentence to help me understand and remember.	○	○	○	○	○
I try to understand and remember by creating a picture in my mind.	○	○	○	○	○
I try to remember the sound of the new language.	○	○	○	○	○
I think of similar words or language I have encountered.	○	○	○	○	○
I think about what I know about the topic area, and this helps me understand.	○	○	○	○	○
I use my knowledge of my own language or other languages to help me understand.	○	○	○	○	○

resource sheet

2

S

Assessing strategic competence in listening (contd)

	always	often	sometimes	rarely	never
I try to guess the meaning from the context.	○	○	○	○	○
I work with a partner or in a group to practise the new language.	○	○	○	○	○
I ask my teacher to repeat or explain the unfamiliar language or sounds.	○	○	○	○	○

2. Can you think of any other ways you learn to listen? How often do you use these methods?

    ....
    ....
    ....
    ....

3. What do you find easy or difficult about listening in French/German/ Spanish?

    ....
    ....
    ....
    ....

4. How do you try to improve your listening?

    ....
    ....
    ....
    ....

5. What do you think are the best ways to learn to listen in a foreign language? Why?

    ....
    ....
    ....
    ....

resource sheet

Appendix 2:
Interpreter training

Introduction

Mention the word 'interpreter' to a linguist and he or she might immediately think of high-level conferences at international level. In such settings, highly trained specialists show an amazing ability to operate between two languages, simultaneously listening to one language and speaking in another. At first sight, therefore, this very high level of specialist skill might not seem immediately relevant to developing listening skills in the sixth form. When interpreters are trained, they already have advanced competence in language skills, which they then have to adapt to the particular demands of their profession.

However, teachers might reasonably feel that they could draw from the experience of interpreter training and apply some of the techniques to their classroom practice. **Simultaneous** interpreting is not a skill likely to be developed in classrooms and has therefore not been included in this contribution. But all language speakers engage, at some time, in **consecutive** interpreting. This is the activity where the speaker pauses at the end of each sentence or speech group to allow the interpreter to offer a version in the other language. As a classroom activity, possibly with a Foreign Language Assistant, this sort of task is highly relevant in developing habits of paying close attention, quick thinking and selecting key information and taking notes. It is true that, at A level, only one Board (Edexcel) actually has an Interpreting option in the oral exam. But after A level, ad hoc interpreting may be the most common activity a person with a command of a foreign language is asked to perform.

The following contributions on training and testing the skills of interpreting are to be considered within this general context. The first piece is written by two specialists in the field: Jiang Hong, a United Nations interpreter in English–Chinese and Dr Robert Neather, Assistant Professor of Translation in the

Department of Chinese, Translation and Linguistics at City University, Hong Kong.

The second piece gives more details about the Edexcel A level option in Interpreting, drawing attention to the classroom preparation required, to the demands of consecutive interpreting in the exam itself, and the need to listen for detail and render such details accurately.

Case study

Training the ears of interpreters
Jiang Hong and Dr Robert Neather

- -

Input

Interpretation, as a means of transmitting messages from one language to another, begins with the input end of the process, which may include anything from background knowledge to venue layout. But the pivotal point begins when the speaker starts his or her speech and the interpreter begins to listen. What the interpreter captures, either in memory or notes, will be the essential element determining the outcome of the interpreting process.

Words or message?

What students suffer most when leqrning to interpret is the so-called 'gravitational pull' of the source language. This means that they might be pulled too much towards the detail of the language, so that at the end of the listening process what has been captured would be a conglomerate of words and sounds, but a weak logical structure (if any structure at all!) to put them into messages that convey meaning. The logical link, like the string that threads the pearls into a necklace, has been lost.

This may be a result of several problematic elements that can be frustrating not only at the listening comprehension stage but also at various other stages of interpretation. The first and most obvious difficulty is linguistic, including new words, involved sentence structures, unusual expressions, etc. The second is speech-related features such as accent, speed and noise. The third is content-related, i.e. subject matter which is not familiar to the students.

A useful exercise to help students tune their ears toward meaning, logic and the message is **paraphrasing**. What the students should be encouraged to capture is the object or message which a certain word, phrase or paragraph points to, instead of the direct linguistic equivalent in the target language. For example, at the most basic word level, the interpreter may be required to translate the German word *Baum* into English. Listening comprehension points to the image or concept of a tree, which will then in turn lead to the linguistic equivalent in English, the word 'tree'. Failing, however, to come up with the exact linguistic equivalent, there is still the understood concept to work on and to interpret into a synonym or even into a longer explanatory phrase. By trying to express the same concept and message using alternative words, phrases, or sentence structures, the students are tackling the same object or message from different angles and will feel the freedom of expression from the source language, thus gaining confidence in their ability to take control of the comprehension and interpreting process. Such an approach can potentially be applied to language units of any size: in a complex account of a ministerial meeting, for instance, it is essential that the interpreter extract from all the verbiage the key facts as to who said what, what was decided, etc. It is sometimes said, therefore, that the interpreter's mind works in a kind of 'telegrammatic' way, compressing the original speech into a set of essential information which is then 'reconstituted' in the target language.

In training students to focus on messages, analysis of the source text is an important tool, for it allows students to unearth the logic of a discourse without the pressure of time as is the case in listening comprehension. They should get into the habit of asking such questions as 'What are the indispensable words in the text?', 'What are the key messages, supportive messages and negligible messages?', 'What is the sequence of reasoning of the writer in making his or her argument?', etc. This, as we shall see below, will also be instrumental in developing note-taking skills.

While trying to break away from the gravitational pull of the source language, over-emphasis on the effort of breaking away, particularly in the case of beginners, may result in over-reaction, with a danger of totally ignoring the register, style and rhetorical features of the original speech. The way in which an idea is put across can sometimes be just as important as the meaning itself. Thus it is important that the need to grasp messages does not result in insensitivity to the style and choice of words, and thus in the loss of important nuances. The tendency of over-/under-paraphrasing should therefore be checked from the beginning. Though a fine line to tread, it is indispensable should the interpreter wish to be a faithful messenger.

Useful exercises

Preparation and prediction

To remove impediments and make the listening-comprehension process into a solid preparation and feeding operation for the ensuing interpretation process, several exercises may prove to be very useful. Linguistically, it is advisable to give the students a glossary related to the speech they are to interpret. This not only helps students with the language, but also prepares them psychologically for what sounds may strike their ear drums when the speech actually begins. Reading the vocabulary aloud can be very useful in the familiarisation process. It is also extremely helpful if students are given a briefing on the broad background of the subject matter, or even given a written text on the related subject. With this preparation, the students have the basic knowledge to relate to the logic and discussions of the speech. This also helps the students psychologically by giving them an idea of what to expect, and the ability to predict, which is one of the skills that interpreters rely on to handle the interpreting process.

TAKING NOTES

Note-taking is one of the basic skills for an interpreter in the consecutive setting. Notes serve as a reminder and guide in the interpreter's effort to reformulate in the target language the message just expressed by the speaker. As a reminder, what has been scribbled down on the note pad must function not as a word-for-word record of the source language but rather as a clue to a string of meaning that is still lingering on in the interpreter's active memory. To serve this purpose, the interpreter may learn or develop his or her own system of abbreviations and signs, a sort of shorthand, or adopt those already established, to save time and lessen the burden of writing. It takes practice to internalise the system into an active realm of writing.

As a guide, the notes should point to the direction of the discourse, be it an emphasis, a turn of argument or a cause–effect relationship, to name just a few. If the flow of discourse is similar to the flow of traffic, words such as 'but', 'therefore', 'furthermore', 'for example', 'first of all', etc, function like traffic lights and signs that direct the flow. When these signposts are well positioned and laid out in the notes, then the interpreting will flow smoothly.

The physical layout of notes is often used to reflect the logical structure of messages heard and understood. Indentation is the most popular practice, by which a major argument or a headline message is noted down against the left-hand edge of the page, and supportive or subordinate messages noted underneath with an indentation. To denote the completion of one message unit, a line is usually drawn under the notes, so the next space is understood to be containing a fresh message unit. A note pad should preferably be of a size that is easy to hold with one hand; a common practice is to divide each page into two columns, with notes taken first in one column and then in the other, thus encouraging a more vertical layout. The way in which the different points within a given broad message group are written down and arranged on the page can often take a quite visual form. For example, suppose we use the symbol □ to mean 'a country', and $ to denote money or investment, then the idea that 'there is investment pouring into this country' might be simply written as $→ □ (while 'funds flowing out of this country' might be: $□→). Thus, sometimes, an interpreter's notes for each portion of a speech may resemble a kind of miniature mind map, in which we see again that the interpreter attempts to detach him- or herself from the words of the original text. However, it should be stressed that every interpreter develops his or her own style of note-taking – there is no single 'correct' approach.

In training, a good slow-motion exercise to start with would be for students to work on a given text. Key words that serve as reminders and guides should be highlighted. Then they can be transferred to a note pad, with a proper physical layout to reflect the logical relations as well as the message units. The third step could be the replacement of words with whatever signs that may simplify the writing task, such as 'x' for 'but', 'however', 'nevertheless', etc. When students become comfortable with the idea of a logical physical layout and their own sign system, they could be put to more rigorous exercises of real-time note-taking. Note-taking can also be usefully practised 'intra-lingually': the teacher can read a text in the mother tongue and ask students to take notes and then 'interpret' the message back in the same language. In this way, with no added language difficulties, concentration is focused on practising note-taking skills, and on developing the right balance between short-term memory and notes that is essential for interpreting – because notes, we should stress again, are only reminders and should not be relied on to excess.

Dealing with accents and individual variations

Constant exposure is probably the most effective way of coping with difficult accents. Accents of native speakers are more related to pronunciation, while non-native speakers may be heavily influenced by their mother tongue, not only phonetically but also grammatically and in discourse. Familiarisation with these accents and some knowledge of the speaker's mother tongue may relieve the interpreter of the perplexity of wondering 'what on earth is he talking about?'. The process is much like voice recognition by computers. The computer must be trained to understand the speech of a certain speaker so as to recognise *se-hui* or *tsi tsa* of a Chinese speaker with a southern accent to mean, in fact, *she-hui* (society) and *chi cha* (have tea) respectively in standard Mandarin. The same is true with training the ears of interpreters who have to deal with all sorts of accents, for example, of the English-speaking world, ranging from Indian to Australian English to 'Singlish'.

Concluding remarks

This article has touched briefly on some basic issues that need to be dealt with when initiating students into the profession of interpreting. It is by no means exhaustive and only serves only as a reference for listening-comprehension training. The authors would be very pleased if some of the elements could be adapted to more general language learning.

Case study

Interpreting as a teaching tool
Peter L. Willig, Chair of German, Edexcel

- -

Introduction

Edexcel introduced an interpreting test at A level in French, German and Spanish six years ago in its legacy syllabus. With the revision of the AS/A2 specifications introduced in 2002, the Interpreting examination continued at A2 level in the three languages as an option set against the Oral discussion of issues. Centres may enter candidates for either option on an individual basis: it is not compulsory for all students in a teaching cohort to be entered for either the Interpreting option or the Oral discussion of issues.

Since its introduction, the Interpreting option has become increasingly popular and each year has attracted an ever larger entry. Many centres have devoted a considerable amount of time and effort in devising and developing appropriate teaching strategies in the skills required for the examination. Every year Edexcel mounts a number of INSET support courses where inter alia teaching strategies, the rationale of the examination and assessment procedures are considered.

Examination format

The format of the examination is very straightforward. Students are required to act as interpreter between two interlocutors, neither of whom speaks the other's language. The candidate renders consecutively in the appropriate language the utterances of the two interlocutors who read from a transcription of the conversation. The scenarios of the interpreting tasks are all authentic and reflect the cultural context of the countries and communities of the target language. All the situations for the tests are drawn from one of the following topic areas: school/college, the world of work, business, leisure and travel.

The examination, which is timed to last fifteen minutes, takes place during a designated week in May. The tests are recorded and sent to an Edexcel examiner for assessment. For each examination two topic areas are chosen on a cyclical basis and two tests which are closely related to each other are devised on each of the topics. The two tests on the same topic area differ in specific detail and the use of certain expressions. Four tests are therefore set for each examination session, which are used on specific dates in the order prescribed by Edexcel.

After a brief introduction in which the formalities are exchanged (e.g. *Guten Tag, Bonjour*, etc), candidates proceed to transmit consecutively each section of the test into the appropriate language. The sections are all semantically self-contained and vary marginally in length. For example, one interlocutor may reply to a comment of the other interlocutor with the short phrase: 'You are right'. An example of a longer utterance might be: 'He wasn't able to catch the 10.15 train'. Here again, the phrase represents a self-contained semantic unit although it is slightly longer. Places in the scenario where the interlocutors must pause to allow students time to interpret are indicated by a bar [|] in the text: the pauses occur at meaningful points in the interchange.

Students may ask for a section to be repeated in which case the interlocutors must repeat the section exactly as written. Candidates may also ask for occasional clarification of words and structures with which they are unfamiliar, and the interlocutor is permitted to explain in the relevant language the meaning of the phrase or word unknown by the student. For example, if a student does not know the German word *Stadtverwaltung* the examiner may explain the concept in his or her own words within the context of the dialogue. The amount of repetition and clarification demanded by the student is reflected in the final assessment.

Each test is carefully devised to encompass a gradation of difficulty. The interpreting test is not one of translation; it is essentially one of transmission. In other words, the determining criteria are how successfully the student conveys both the information and the linguistic reference of the original statement into the relevant language.

Teaching for the interpreting test

When it comes to teaching for the test it is advisable to start by preparing students in the necessary skills of interpreting at least six months before the examination. Students must first be taught to react quickly and intuitively to a large number of set phrases in both languages and render these appropriately in the relevant language. 'Stereotype' phrases figure in discourse situations with varying degrees of frequency and students should be familiarised with these from the start. Such phrases in French and German are inter alia: *Ça dépend/Das kommt darauf an/Depende; Je suis désolé/Das tut mir Leid/Lo siento; Ich habe keine Ahnung/Je n'ai aucune idée/No tengo ningún idea; Ich muss/Il faut que.../Hay que ...'*. The structure of various common verbs and idioms also occur from time to time in many interchanges. An exemplification of this is the structure in French and German of *wollen/vouloir* in statements such as 'He wants you to ring him this evening': *Er will, dass du ihn heute Abend anrufst/Il veut que tu l'appelles ce soir.*

Experience has shown that it is far simpler for students to transmit the utterances of each interlocutor as spoken rather than resort, for example, to the reported speech mode. This is particularly the case when transmitting into the target language where some confusion may arise. For example, if the statement to be transmitted is: 'Have you any children?' it is much more straightforward for candidates to render this as spoken, e.g. *Haben Sie Kinder?/Vous avez des enfants?* rather than *Er möchte gern wissen, ob Sie Kinder haben/hätten/Il voudrait savoir si vous avez des enfants*. It is, of course, not wrong to use the reported speech mode and candidates are not penalised for this, but in general centres have found it more natural for the flow of the dialogue to train candidates to transmit utterances exactly as spoken by both interlocutors.

Students also require practice in the use of qualifiers and intensifiers to convey the essential meaning of the original. 'It was quite interesting' rendered as *c'était très intéressant/es war sehr interessant*, is clearly inappropriate, as it does not convey the substance of the original. In order to transmit the original utterance more effectively it is important to acquaint students with qualifiers and intensifiers such as: *surtout/vor allem/sobre todo; assez/ziemlich/bastante; exactement/genau/exactamente; environ/ungefähr/aproximadamente*.

Factual correctness is also central to the exercise. For example *Die Stadt hat genau zwanzig Grundschulen* rendered as 'There are roughly twenty schools in the area' does not convey the correct facts as given in the English statement. Similarly *Le train arrivera à trois heures moins le quart* as 'The train arrived at 3.15' is factually incorrect.

Exemplifications of appropriate transmission

Discussion of the appropriateness of various phrases plays an important role in the teaching methodology. An effective way of doing this is to take a core phrase and then look at potentially acceptable and unacceptable renderings.

Below are two examples in French and German of renditions of an English utterance:

'I have no idea what his monthly salary is.'

1. *J'ignore combien il gagne par mois.*
2. *Je ne sais pas combien d'argent il fait.*
3. *Je ne suis pas sûr combien d'argent il touche chaque mois.*
4. *Son salaire est bas.*
5. *C'est impossible à dire s'il est riche.*

The first rendition conveys the sense of the original effectively, whereas the second omits an important element. The third statement is authentic, idiomatic and factually accurate, whereas the fourth and fifth renditions do not render essential information contained in the original statement.

'Although he liked the job at first, he now finds it very boring.'

1. *Obwohl er anfangs seinen Job mochte, findet er ihn jetzt sehr langweilig.*
2. *Zuerst fand er seinen Job gut aber jetzt ist er ihm total langweilig.*
3. *Die Arbeit war gut aber jetzt ist die Arbeit nicht so gut.*
4. *Zuerst war er glücklich mit seinem Job aber jetzt nicht.*
5. *Er hasst seinen Job heute.*

The first two renditions convey all the necessary information of the original appropriately. In the second example, it should be noted that the subordinate clause is not necessary to convey the meaning of the original statement, as the exercise is one of transmission and not one of word-for-word translation. The main criterion is whether or not this rendition conveys the correct information and spirit of the original, and in the second statement this is clearly the case. The third statement is characterised by a lack of precision and the German rendition is only partial. Similarly, the fourth example is incomplete. Statement five is a poor and largely inaccurate paraphrase of the original utterance.

Student performance and reaction

Candidates who select the option manifest considerable commitment to the activity and most have revealed a commendable degree of proficiency in the interpreting skills they have acquired during the course. Candidates experience comparatively few problems in rendering the target language into English but occasionally a few students, whose command of the target language – particularly in terms of grammatical, syntactical and morphological accuracy – is somewhat insecure, may experience some problems of communication.

The Interpreting option prepares candidates very effectively in a practical, marketable and highly relevant skill, which can be applied to a variety of authentic situations. Students themselves recognise clearly the relevance of the activity and pursue the course with commendable enthusiasm. Several students have found posts in a variety of professions where, post-A2 level, they can use the skill and a number have gone on to pursue courses of Practical Interpreting and Translation at university level.

For further information, please see **www.edexcel.org.uk**.

Appendix 3:
Selected sources of listening material on the Internet

Radio

The BBC World Service website (**www.bbc.co.uk/worldservice/index.shtml**) has news broadcasts in 43 languages, and the ILGRadio: International Broadcasting Web Directory (**www.ilgradio.com/ibwd/ilg–ibwd.htm#ES**) provides an excellent and comprehensive list of links to worldwide broadcasting stations, including local, national and international stations. Other key radio stations found on the Internet include:

French

RFI – Radio France International – **www.rfi.fr**
Radio France – **www.radiofrance.fr**
Radio Canada International – **www.rcinet.ca**

German

Deutsche Welle Radio – **www.dw-world.de**
DeutschlandRadio Berlin (DLR) and Deutschlandfunk (DLF) – **www.dradio.de**
ORF Austrian Radio – **www.orf.at**
Westdeutscher Rundfunk (Köln) – **www.wdr.de/radio**

Russian

Voice of Russia – **www.vor.ru**
Radio 101 – **www.101.ru**
Radio Echo of Moscow – **www.echo.msk.ru/efir**
Radio Mayak – **www.radiomayak.ru**
Radio Rossia – **www.radiorus.ru**

Spanish

Radio Nacional de España – **www.rtve.es/rne**
REE – Radio Exterior de España – **www.rtve.es/rne/ree**
Cadena 100 – **www.cadena100.es**

Television

French

France 2 – **www.france2.fr**
TV5 – **www.tv5.org**
MTV – **www.mtv.fr**

German

ntv – **www.ntv.de**
ARD – **www.ard.de** and **www.tagesschau.de**
ZDF – **www.zdf.de**
RTL – **www.rtl.de**
SAT 1 – **www.sat1.de**
3Sat – **www.3sat.de**
MTV – **www.mtv.de**

Russian

TV1 – **www.1tv.ru**
NTV.RU – **www.ntv.ru**
NETTV – **www.nettv.ru**

Spanish

Antena 3 – **www.antena3tv.com**
MTV – **www.mtv.es**

References

Brown, G. (1986) 'Investigating listening comprehension in context'. *Applied Linguistics*, 7: 3, 284–302.

Byrnes, H (1984) 'The role of listening comprehension: A theoretical base'. *Foreign Language Annals*, 17, 317–329.

Cutler, A. and Swinney, D. A. (1987) 'Prosody and the development of comprehension'. *Journal of Child Language*, 14: 1, 145–167.

Gerrig, R. J. and Murphy, G. L. (1992) 'Contextual influences on the comprehension of complex concepts'. In: Oakhill, J. and Garnham, A. (eds) (1992) *Language and Cognitive Processes. Special Issue: Discourse Representation and Text Processing*' 7: 3–4, 205–230.

Hattie, J., Biggs, J. and Purdie, N. (1996) 'Effects of learning skills intervention on student learning. A meta-analysis'. *Review of Educational Research*, 66: 2, 99–136.

Hayashi, T. (1991) 'Interactive processing of words in connected speech in L1 and L2'. *IRAL*, 29: 2, 151–160.

Jones, B. (2001) Advanced Pathfinder 2: *Developing learning strategies*. CILT.

Kelly, P. (1991) 'Lexical ignorance: the main obstacle to listening comprehension with advanced foreign language learners'. *IRAL*, 29: 2, 135–149.

Kleist, H. (1805) 'Über die allmählige Verfertigung der Gedanken beim Reden' [On the gradual preparation of thought during speech]. In: K. Müller-Salget (ed) *Sämtliche Werke und Briefe in vier Bänden, Bd. 3: Erzählungen, Anekdoten, Gedichte, Schriften*, 534– 540. Frankfurt/Main: Deutscher Klassiker Verlag.

Koda, K. (1988) 'Cognitive process in second language reading'. *Second Language Research*, 4: 2, 133–156.

Langs, R. L. (1978) *The listening process*. New York: Jason Aronson.

Liberman, A. M. (1970) 'Some characteristics of perception in the speech mode. Perception and its disorders', 48, 238–254. Discrimination in speech and nonspeech modes. *Cognitive Psychology*, 2, 131–157.

Markham, P. L. (1988) 'Gender and perceived expertness of the speaker as factors in ESL listening recall'. *TESOL Quarterly*, 22, 397–406

McLachlan, A. (2001) Advanced Pathfinder 1: *Advancing oral skills.* CILT.

Neather, T. (2001) Advanced Pathfinder 3: *Tests and targets.* CILT.

Noordman, L. G. M. and Vonk, W. (1992) 'Readers' knowledge and the control of inferences in reading'. In: Oakhill, J. and Garnham, A. (eds) (1992) *Language and Cognitive Processes. Special Issue: Discourse Representation and Text Processing*, 7: 3–4, 373–392.

O'Malley, J. M. (1987) 'The effects of training in the use of learning strategies on learning English as a second language'. In: Wenden, A. and Rubin, J. (eds) (1987) *Learner strategies in language learning*. Prentice Hall.

O'Malley, J. M., Chamot, A. U. and Küpper, L. (1989) 'Listening comprehension strategies in second language acquisition'. *Applied Linguistics*, 10: 4, 418–437.

Oxford, R. L. (1990) *Language learning strategies: What every teacher should know*. New York: Newbury House.

Oxford, R. L. (1993) 'Research update on teaching L2 listening'. *System*, 21: 2, 205–211.

Richards, J. C. (1983) 'Listening comprehension: Approach, design, procedure'. *TESOL Quarterly*, 17, 2: 219–239.

Rinvolucri, M. (1981) 'Empathetic listening'. In: The British Council (1981) *The teaching of listening comprehension* 15–19. ELT Documents Special. The British Council.

Riseborough, M. G. (1981) 'Physiographic gestures as decoding facilitators: Three experiments exploring a neglected facet of communication'. *Journal of Nonverbal Behavior*, 5, 172–183.

Rost, M. (1990) *Listening in language learning*. Longman.

Rost, M. (1991) *Listening in action*. Prentice Hall.

Rubin, J. (1994) 'A review of second language listening comprehension research'. *The Modern Language Journal*, 78: 2, 199–221.

Tang, H. N. and Moore, D. W. (1992) 'Effects of cognitive and metacognitive pre-reading activities on the reading comprehension of ESL learners'. *Educational Psychology*, 12: 3–4, 315–331.

Treisman, A. (1960). 'Verbal cues, language, and meaning in selective attention'. *Quarterly Journal of Experimental Psychology*, 12: 242–248.

Treisman, A. (1964) 'Monitoring and storage of irrelevant messages in selective attention'. *Journal of Verbal Learning and Verbal Behavior*, 3, 449–459.

Turner, K. (1995) Pathfinder 21: *Listening in a foreign language. A skill we take for granted?*. CILT.

Ur, P. (1984) *Teaching listening comprehension*. Cambridge University Press.

Vanderplank, R. (1988) 'Implications of differences in native and non-native speaker approaches to listening'. *British Journal of Language Teaching*, 26: 1, 32–41.

Van Patten, B. (1989) 'Can learners attend to form and content while processing input?' *Hispania 72*, 409–417.

Wenden, A. (1987) 'Incorporating learner training in the classroom'. In: Wenden, A. and Rubin, J. (eds) (1987) *Learner strategies in language learning*. Prentice Hall. 159–167.

Wilkinson, A., Stratta, L. and Dudley, P. (1974) *The quality of listening*. The report of the Schools Council Oracy Project. Macmillan.

Further reading

General

Anderson, A. and Lynch, T. (1988) *Listening*. Oxford University Press.

Carter, D. (2003) New Pathfinder 2: *The language of success: Improving grades at GCSE*. CILT.

Chambers, G. (2001) Reflections on Practice 6: *Reflections on motivation*. CILT.

Dole, J. A. et al (1991) 'Moving from the old to the new: Research on reading comprehension instruction'. *Review of Educational Research*, 61: 2, 239–264.

Ellis, R. (1994) *The study of second language acquisition*. Oxford University Press.

Fawkes, S. (1998) *Switched on?* Multilingual Matters.

Gleitman, L. R. and Wanner, E. (1982) 'Language acquisition: the state of the state of the art'. In: Wanner, E. and Gleitman, L. R. (1982) *Language acquisition: the state of the art*. 3–48. New York: Cambridge University Press.

Graham, S. (1997) *Effective language learning*. Multilingual Matters.

Green, S., Haworth, S., Doublier, M. (1998) *On est fou du foot/Football crazy*. CILT.

Green, S. (2000) (ed) *New perspectives on teaching and learning modern languages*. Multilingual Matters.

Luria, A. R. (1981) *Language and cognition*. Washington, DC: V. H. Winston.

McDonough, S. (1995) *Strategy and skill in learning a foreign language*. Edward Arnold.

Moray, N. (1969) *Listening and attention*. Penguin.

A level listening materials

French

AS level/A level French listening comprehension practice tests. Mechani, D. and Rodmell, I. Authentik. www.authentik.com (published annually).

Authentik en français. Dublin: Authentik (published five times per year).

Champs Elysées (La France en CD et cassette). Audio-magazine (11 issues p.a.).

Communiquez. Noel, M.-F. and Davies, V. (1999) Hodder & Stoughton.

Dossiers France télévision. Bishop, G., Dyson, P. and Worth, V. (1995) John Murray.

Ecoute – écoute. Carton, F. et al. (1986) Paris: Didier (for CRAPEL). European Schoolbooks (distributor). www.eurobooks.co.uk.

Eurolab français plus. Revilo Language Cards (1994).

Je t'écoute!: intermediate listening practice. Marsden, R. (1995) John Murray.

Jeunes de France (1993) Cambridge University Press.

La parole aux Français. Padfield, D. (2000) Language Centre Publications.

Linguaphone Daily Services (2003) www.linguaphone.com/dailyservices.

Micro dans la rue. Padfield, D. and Smith, M. (1999) Language Centre Publications.

UniS-talk!: French. Thacker, M. (ed) (2000) University of Surrey, European Language Teaching Centre.

Vidéo France. Rey, J. N. (1990) Paris: Hatier. European Schoolbooks (distributor).

German

Aktuelles aus Radio und Presse. Eckhard-Long, C. (1989) Nelson.

Authentik AS/A level German listening comprehension practice tests. Murray, U. and Sudrow, B. Dublin: Authentik. www.authentik.com (published annually).

Authentik auf Deutsch. Dublin: Authentik (published five times per year).

Deutschlandspiegel/The German scene and *Prisma: the arts magazine on video.* German Film and Video Library.

Eurolab Deutsch plus. (1994) Revilo Language Cards.

Jung in Deutschland. (1993) Cambridge University Press. (Video Profiles)

Paß mal auf!: intermediate listening practice. Marsden, R. (1996) John Murray.

Schau ins Land. (2000) The German language audiomagazine Nashville (USA). Champs Elysées (11 issues p.a.).

TV Aktuell. McAleavy, M. (2000) Oxford University Press.

Turbo. (2000) Bonn: InterNationes.

Turbo. (2001). 4 Learning.

UniS-talk!: German. Thacker, M. (ed) (2000) University of Surrey, European Language Teaching Centre.

Russian

The learnables. Book 4. International Linguistics Corporation. Kansas City, Missouri: www.learnables.com.

Listening exercises: http://masterrussian.com.

Spanish

¡Andaluces antes de todo!. Poitiers: Centre Régional de Documentation Pédagogique de Poitiers. 1989–90. Grant and Cutler (distributor).

AS/A level listening comprehension practice tests (Spanish). Dublin: Authentik. www.authentik.com (published annually).

Authentik en español. Dublin: Authentik (published five times per year).

Como suena: materiales para la comprensión auditiva. Miquel, L. and Sans, N. (1991) Madrid: Difusión. European Schoolbooks (distributor).

España hoy. (1994) Cambridge University Press.

La escucha: comprensión oral. Palencia, R. (1992) Madrid: Ediciones SM.

Puerta del sol: the Spanish language audio-magazine. Champs Elysées.

UniS-talk!: Spanish. Thacker, M. (ed) (2000) University of Surrey, European Language Teaching Centre.